THE BRIVIARY

A BOOK OF FAMILY PRAYER

BERTILLA DORIS

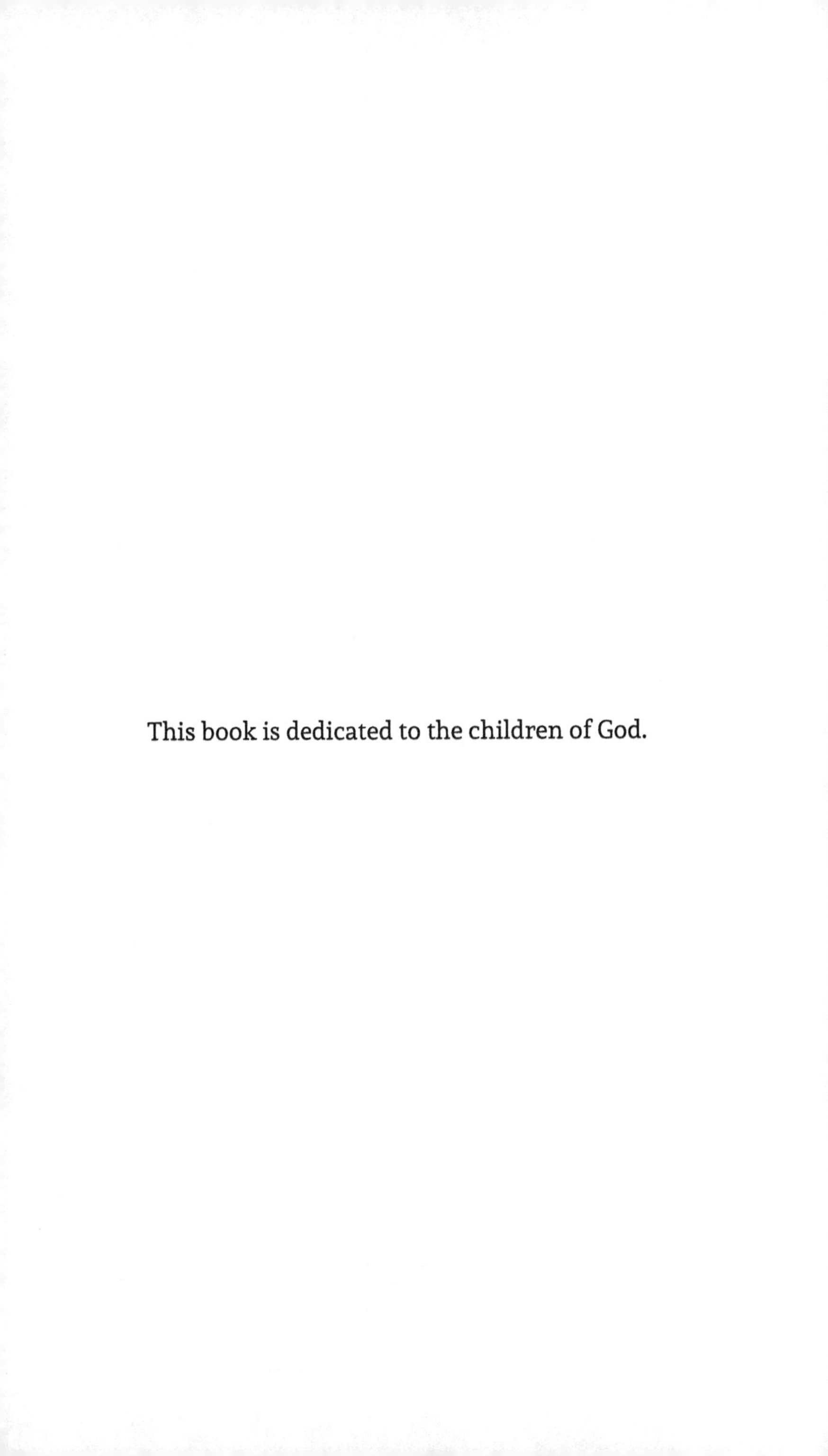

This book is dedicated to the children of God.

Contents

Contents

Foreword

This expanded prayer book is intended for the many young people outdoors who are in need of one. We anticipate being able to provide comparable prayer booklets very shortly. There are no canonical family or private prayers in the Orthodox faith. All of the prayers of the Church are intended to be recited in churches or monasteries. I'm not aware of any Church law requiring laypeople to pray seven times each day or to recite all the qaumas. The prayers in the current book were picked at random for both individual and communal usage. Any constructive criticism is appreciated. The various versions of the Lord's Prayer are all worthwhile. Some of the supplementary prayers are intended for use at meetings and conferences as well as in solitary meditation. We all need God's assistance to improve our prayer lives and become nearer to Him.

WHAT IS PRAYER? WHY PRAY? HOW PRAY?

1. What is Prayer ?

To pray is to breathe. We cannot survive if we do not breathe. Air enters our lungs when breathing, purifying our blood by removing carbon dioxide from it and replenishing it with oxygen. I expire after a few minutes of not breathing. I require more air when I'm working out than when I'm sleeping or sitting in a chair. Thankfully, God has decreed that we do not perish spiritually simply because we have neglected to pray for while. But without prayer, sin builds up and interferes with the regular operation of the spiritual life. Additionally, you need more prayer than usual if you have vital spiritual tasks to complete.The only people who regularly exercise their spiritual muscles are those who pray. Prayer is connection with God, a channel through which we can communicate with Him and receive His love. We may become more like God by intentionally being in this loving connection. Through prayer, we develop qualities that are more like God: love, wisdom, strength, kindness, and goodness. We are purified of the accumulated pollutants of life via prayer, and we are given the strength to live a good, kind, and holy life. Prayer is not a matter of asking God for all kinds of things. Some teenagers only contact their earthly father when they want financial assistance.

When it comes to our heavenly Father, we shouldn't behave like they did and only turn to Him when we are in need. As with any real love, the connection has value in and of itself. What important is not what we get from it, nonetheless, that we have a close relationship with our kind

Heavenly Father.

2. Why Pray?

Does God not already be aware of our needs before we ever ask him? He wants us to inquire as to why. Does prayer in any way alter God's will? Can God's predetermined future be altered by my prayer? These are valid inquiries that call for an answer. "Your Father knows what you need before you ask Him," the Bible states clearly (Mathew 6:8). God, however, wants us to be aware of what is best for both ourselves and others. God desires that our wills do not go toward evil but rather have a strong desire for good. As a result, prayer is a tool for developing a desire for good and for directing our wills toward the source of all good, which is God. Thus, utilising our freedom to turn toward and choose the good, prayer is a method to become good. We can become like God through praying. God is kind and wants good to happen. Like God, we need to want and will that which is good. We learn to seek the good that God also desires through having communication with God. God said "Let there be light," and light appeared. And God observed the lovely light (Gen. 1:3-4). God's plans came to pass. The goal is to imitate God. As a result, in order for the good to happen as we wish, we must also have the ability to will it. As we get closer to God, this will happen. Prayer is a way for us to communicate our desire for the realisation of the good. Our prayers will resemble God's creative Word more when we are freed from selfishness, pride, and bad desires. God's creative Word can generate light just by saying "let there be light." We now possess a portion of God's divine essence. He has invited us to participate in God's own perfection and splendour (2 Pet. 1:4).

We are changed into the image of God and given access to His omnipotent power when we put our faith in Him and live a life of obedience, prayer, worship, virtue, knowledge, godliness, brotherly affection, and love (2 Peter 1:5-8).

God desires for us to participate in the process of reshaping our world via knowledge and prayer. By prayer we do change reality. God has given us that power. But this power is not available to us until we become more god¬ like. That is why the prayers of the saints are more effective than our own prayer— because they are more god-like than we are. If the power to change the world by our will is in the hands of evil men, they will make the world evil. We have to grow in the capacity for prayer by developing the habits of prayer and loving service. And our prayers should not be selfish. In prayer the first focus is God. The second focus is other people.

3. How Pray ?

Prayer has to be learned. It is like swim¬ ming. Whenyou are first thrown into the water, you imy sink. You then may think that the law of gravity is final and cannot be changed. But there are other laws, like those of buoymcy and motion. The mere knowledge ofthese laws cannot teach you to swim. On; jumps in and slowly, by repeated pracice, acquires the skills of remaining afloatand of moving on the surface of or under tbs water. And some people are more skiful swimmers than others, because they lave learned the rules and acquired the skills by constant practice.

The first rule in prayer as in swimming, is not to give up just because you do notsucceed in the first three or four attempts. Prayer is a spiritual skill to be acquired by constant practice.

The second rule, again as in swimming, is to "let go" to let the water support you, to be unanxious and relaxed. In prayer also we have to let ourselves go, relax, trust in God to support you and teach you how to pray.

The third rule is to keep up the practice, even if you do not feel like it, enjoy it. In the life of prayer, our inheren; love of sensual pleasures and our selfish love of laziness and comfort, will interefere to make us reluctant to keep up the practice finding various excuses for not praying.

A fourth rule, closely connected with the third, is : develop the discipline of prayer through fasting and self-control. Man does not become free and good like God until he learns to control his own inner drives and passions.

A fifth rule is to use our whole body and even material things in the service of prayer. Prayer is an act of the whole man, body, soul and spirit—not simply an act of the mind.

A sixth rule is to keep the balance between group prayer and personal prayer. Man is not primarily an individual. It is as a member of the Body of Christ that he has any standing before God.

The Holy Mass

The central act of worship of the Roman Catholic Church, which culminates in celebration of the sacrament of the Eucharist

1

Order Of The Mass

The Introductory Rites

The Introductory Rites help the faithful come together as one, establish communion and prepare themselves properly to listen to the Word of God and to celebrate the Eucharist worthily.

All stand. *The Priest approaches the altar with the ministers and venerates it while the Entrance Song is sung*

Sign of the Cross

P: In the name of the Father, and of the Son, and of the Holy Spirit.

L: Amen.

Greeting

P: The grace of our Lord Jesus Christ, and the love of God, and the communion of the Holy Spirit be with you all.

L: And with your spirit.

The Priest, or a Deacon, or another minister, may very briefly introduce the faithful to the Mass of the day.

Penitential Act

P: Brethren (brothers and sisters), let us acknowledge our sins, and so prepare ourselves to celebrate the sacred mysteries.

A brief pause for silence follows, and then one of the following Penitential Acts:

All say:

L: I confess to almighty God and to you, my brothers and sisters, that I have greatly sinned, in my thoughts and in my words, in what I have done and in what I have failed to do, And, striking their breast, they say: through my fault, through my fault, through my most grievous fault; therefore I ask blessed Mary ever-Virgin, all the Angels and Saints, and you, my brothers and sisters, to pray for me to the Lord our God.

The absolution by the Priest follows:

P: May almighty God have mercy on us, forgive us our sins, and bring us to everlasting life.

L: Amen.

The Kyrie

The Kyrie, eleison (Lord, have mercy) invocations may follow:

P: Lord, have mercy.

L: Lord, have mercy.

P: Christ, have mercy.

L: Christ, have mercy.

P: Lord, have mercy.

L: Lord, have mercy.

The Gloria

When indicated this hymn is either sung or said.

Glory to God in the highest, and on earth peace to people of good will. We praise you, we bless you, we adore you, we glorify you, we give you thanks for your great glory, Lord God, heavenly King, O God, almighty Father. Lord Jesus Christ, Only Begotten Son, Lord God, Lamb of God, Son of the Father, you take away the sins of the world, have mercy on us; you take away the sins of the world, receive our prayer; you are seated at the right hand of the Father, have mercy on us. For you alone are the Holy One, you alone are the Lord, you alone are the Most High, Jesus Christ, with the Holy Spirit, in the glory of God the Father. Amen.

The Collect

P: Let us pray..........

L: Amen.

The Liturgy of the Word

All sit

First Reading

To indicate the end of these readings, the reader acclaims:

The word of the Lord.

L: Thanks be to God.

Psalm

Second Reading

On Sundays and certain other days there is a second reading. It concludes with the same responsory as above.

Gospel

P: The Lord be with you.

L: And with your spirit.

P: A reading from the holy Gospel according to N.

He makes the Sign of the Cross on the book and, together with the people, on his forehead, lips, and breast. At the same time the people acclaim:

L: Glory to you, O Lord.

At the end of the Gospel, the Deacon, or the Priest, acclaims:

P: The Gospel of the Lord.

L: Praise to you, Lord Jesus Christ.

All sit

The Homily

At the end of the Homily it is appropriate for there to be a brief silence for recollection. The congregation then stands.

The Creed

On Sundays and Solemnities, the Profession of Faith or Creed will follow. During Lent and Easter Time, especially, the Apostles' Creed may be used.

The Apostles' Creed

I believe in God, the Father almighty, Creator of heaven and earth, and in Jesus Christ, his only Son, our Lord, At the words that follow, up to and including 'the Virgin Mary', all bow. who was conceived by the Holy Spirit, born of the Virgin Mary, suffered under Pontius Pilate, was crucified, died and was buried; he descended into hell; on the third day he rose again from the dead; he ascended into heaven, and is seated at the right hand of God the Father almighty; from there he will come to judge the living and the dead. I believe in the Holy Spirit, the holy catholic Church, the communion of saints, the forgiveness of sins, the resurrection of the body, and life everlasting. Amen.

The Prayer of the Faithful (Bidding Prayers)

The Priest concludes the Prayer with a collect. When the Liturgy of the Word has been completed, the people sit.

The Liturgy of the Eucharist

For Catholics, the Eucharist is the source and summit of the whole Christian life. It is the vital centre of all that the Church is and does, because at its heart is the real presence of the crucified, risen and glorified Lord, continuing and making available his saving work among us.

The Offertory

During the Offertory Song the faithful usually express their participation by making an offering, bringing forward bread and wine for the celebration of the Eucharist and perhaps other gifts to relieve the needs of the Church and of the poor.

When he has received the bread and wine for the celebration, the Priest offers prayer of blessing quietly at the altar. Sometimes these prayers are said aloud. If the priest says the prayers aloud the assembly's acclamation each time is

Blessed be God for ever.

The Priest completes additional personal preparatory rites, and the people rise as he says:

P: Pray, brethren (brothers and sisters), that my sacrifice and yours may be acceptable to God, the almighty Father.

L: May the Lord accept the sacrifice at your hands for the praise and glory of his name, for our good

and the good of all his holy Church.

Then the Priest says the Prayer over the Offerings, at the end of which the people acclaim:

L: Amen.

THE EUCHARISTIC PRAYER

The Eucharistic Prayer, the centre and summit of the entire celebration is a memorial proclamation of praise and thanksgiving for God's work of salvation, a proclamation in which the Body and Blood of Christ are made present by the power of the Holy Spirit and the people are joined to Christ in offering his Sacrifice to the Father.

P: The Lord be with you.

L: And with your spirit.

P: Lift up your hearts.

L: We lift them up to the Lord.

P: Let us give thanks to the Lord our God.

L: It is right and just.

P: It is truly right and just, our duty and our salvation, always and everywhere to give you thanks, Lord, holy Father, almighty and eternal God, through Christ our Lord. His Death we celebrate in love, his Resurrection we confess with living faith, and his Coming in glory we await with unwavering hope. And so, with all the Angels and Saints, we praise you, as without end we acclaim: The Priest concludes the Preface with the people singing or saying aloud:

L: Holy, Holy, Holy Lord God of hosts. Heaven and earth are full of your glory. Hosanna in the highest. Blessed is he who comes in the name of the Lord. Hosanna in the highest.

After the singing of the Sanctus the congregation kneels for the remainder of the Eucharistic Prayer.

P: You are indeed Holy, O Lord, the fount of all holiness. Make holy, therefore, these gifts, we pray, by sending down your Spirit upon them like the dewfall, so that they may become for us the Body and ✠ Blood of our Lord Jesus Christ. At the time he was betrayed and entered willingly into his Passion, he took bread and, giving thanks, broke it, and gave it to his disciples, saying: Take this, all of you, and eat of it, for this is my Body, which will be given up for you. In a similar way, when supper was ended, he took the chalice and, once more giving thanks, he gave it to his disciples, saying: Take this, all of you, and drink from it, for this is the chalice of my Blood, the Blood of the new and eternal covenant, which will be poured out for you and for many for the forgiveness of sins. Do this in memory of me.

After the words of Consecration the priest says:

P: The mystery of faith.

L: We proclaim your Death, O Lord,

and profess your Resurrection

until you come again.

Or:

When we eat this Bread and drink this Cup,

we proclaim your Death, O Lord,

until you come again.

Or:

Save us, Saviour of the world,

for by your Cross and Resurrection

you have set us free.

P: Therefore, as we celebrate the memorial of his Death and Resurrection, we offer you, Lord, the Bread of life and the Chalice of salvation, giving thanks that you have held us worthy to be in your presence and minister to you. Humbly we pray that, partaking of the Body and Blood of Christ, we may be gathered into one by the Holy Spirit. Remember, Lord, your Church, spread throughout the world, and bring her to the fullness of charity, together with N. our Pope and N. our Bishop and all the clergy. Remember also our brothers and sisters who have fallen asleep in the hope of the resurrection, and all who have died in your mercy: welcome them into the light of your face. Have mercy on us all, we pray, that with the Blessed Virgin Mary, Mother of God, with blessed Joseph, her Spouse, with the blessed Apostles, and all the Saints who have pleased you throughout the ages, we may merit to be coheirs to eternal life, and may praise and glorify you through your Son, Jesus Christ.

P: Through him, and with him, and in him, O God, almighty Father, in the unity of the Holy Spirit, all glory and honour is yours, for ever and ever.

L: Amen.

The Communion Rite

The eating and drinking together of the Lord's Body and Blood in a Paschal meal is the culmination of the Eucharist. The themes underlying these rites are the mutual love and reconciliation that are both the condition and the fruit of worthy communion and the unity of the many in the One.

The Lord's Prayer

P: At the Saviour's command and formed by divine teaching, we dare to say:

P&L: Our Father, who art in heaven, hallowed be thy name; thy kingdom come, thy will be done on earth as it is in heaven. Give us this day our daily bread, and forgive us our trespasses, as we forgive those who trespass against us; and lead us not into temptation, but deliver us from evil.

P: Deliver us, Lord, we pray, from every evil, graciously grant peace in our days, that, by the help of your mercy, we may be always free from sin and safe from all distress, as we await the blessed hope and the coming of our Saviour, Jesus Christ.

L: For the kingdom, the power and the glory are yours now and for ever.

P: Lord Jesus Christ, who said to your Apostles: Peace I leave you, my peace I give you, look not on our sins, but on the faith of your Church, and graciously grant her peace and unity in accordance with your will. Who live and reign for ever and ever.

L: Amen.

P: The peace of the Lord be with you always.

L: And with your spirit.

P: Let us offer each other the sign of peace.

And all offer one another the customary sign of peace: a handclasp or handshake, which is an expression of peace, communion, and charity.

Breaking of the Bread

Lamb of God, you take away the sins of the world,
have mercy on us.
Lamb of God, you take away the sins of the world,
have mercy on us.
Lamb of God, you take away the sins of the world,
grant us peace.

After the Lamb of God, the people kneel.

Invitation to Communion

P: Behold the Lamb of God, behold him who takes away the sins of the world. Blessed are those called to the supper of the Lamb.

L: Lord, I am not worthy that you should enter under my roof, but only say the word and my soul shall be healed.

Communion

The Priest says:

The Body (Blood) of Christ.

The communicant replies:

Amen.

After the distribution of Communion, if appropriate, a sacred silence may be observed for a while, or a psalm or other canticle of praise or a hymn may be sung.

Prayer after Communion

P: Let us pray.

All stand and pray in silence. Then the Priest says the Prayer after Communion, at the end of which the people acclaim:

L: Amen.

The Concluding Rites

Any brief announcements to the people follow here. Then the dismissal takes place. Sometimes this takes a more elaborate form than that given below.

Blessing

P: The Lord be with you.

L: And with your spirit.

P: May almighty God bless you, the Father, and the Son, ✠ and the Holy Spirit.

L: Amen.

Dismissal

P: Go forth, the Mass is ended.

Or: Go and announce the Gospel of the Lord.

Or: Go in peace, glorifying the Lord by your life.

Or: Go in peace.

L: Thanks be to God

Hymns

The hymns remind us of our original glory that preceded any "original sin" and remind us of God's intention to see that glory restored in us. The exchange in hymns, then, is vertical – connecting us to God and seeking to hear His voice speaking to our hearts in return. One song is equivalent to 100 prayers, according to an old saying.

2
Index of Hymns

22. God is good
23. God of mercy and compassion
24. God still Loves the World
25. God's love is so wonderful
26. Great and mighty
27. Great indeed are your works
28. Here I am to worship
29. Here we are
30. Hide me now
31. Holy, Holy, Holy Lord
32. Hosanna in the highest
33. How great thou art
34. I have decided to follow Jesus
35. I offer my life
36. I will sing of the mercies
37. Immaculate Mary
38. In his time
39. In the name of Jesus
40. Jingle bell
41. Jingle bell rock
42. Joy to the world
43. Jumbo, Jesus loves you
44. Just like a child
45. Kyrie elesion
46. Listen
47. Living waters
48. Lord have mercy
49. Lord I lift your name on high
50. Make me a channel
51. Making melody
52. Mary's boy child
53. More love, More power
54. Mother of mine

55. O come all ye faithful
56. Power of your love
57. Praise him
58. Rejoice in the Lord, Always
59. Rudolph
60. Save us saviour
61. Seek yee first
62. Shepherd of my soul
63. Shine Jesus Shine
64. Shout to the Lord
65. Showers of blessing
66. Silent night
67. The gift of God
68. This is the day
69. Thy loving Kindness
70. Thy word
71. Walk in the light of the Lord
72. Walking with the Lord
73. We proclaim your death O Lord
74. We shall overcome
75. What a friend we have.
76. Whatsoever you do
77. When we eat
78. You raise me up

3
The Hymns

---

1. All for you
    Ch: All for You Lord, all for You.
Everything I give to You.
All for You Lord, all for You
Make it all your own

Take my hands and feel , Lord
Take them all for You
They are instruments, Lord put them to your use,
To spread your love and give the good news
All for You my God.

Take my joys and sorrows
And the toil of day,
Take my rest and leisure,
All I'll do today, to serve my brothers
Share with them your joy, all for You my God.

Take my mind, my senses,
Feelings and desires, take my will and freedom,
Take my life entire.

I offer You myself and all I love
All for You my God.
2. All to Jesus I surrender
All to Jesus I surrender,
All to Him I freely give;
I will ever love and trust Him,
In His presence daily live.

I surrender all,
I surrender all.
All to Thee, my blessed Savior,
I surrender all.

All to Jesus I surrender,
Humbly at His feet I bow,
Worldly pleasures all forsaken;
Take me, Jesus, take me now.

All to Jesus I surrender,
Make me, Savior, wholly Thine;
Let me feel Thy Holy Spirit,
Truly know that Thou art mine.

All to Jesus I surrender,
Lord, I give myself to Thee;
Fill me with Thy love and power,
Let Thy blessing fall on me.

All to Jesus I surrender,
Now I feel the sacred flame.
Oh, the joy of full salvation!
Glory, glory to His name!

3. As I kneel

As I Kneel Before You,
As I Bow My Head In Prayer,
Take This Day, Make It Yours
And Fill Me With Your Love.
Ave Maria, Gratia Plena,
Dominus Tecum, Benedicta Tu.
All I Have I Give You,
Every Dream And Wish Are Yours,
Mother Of Christ, Mother Of Mine,
Present Them To My Lord.
Ave Maria, Gratia Plena,
Dominus Tecum, Benedicta Tu.
As I Kneel Before You,
And I See Your Smiling Face
Every Thought, Every Word
Is Lost In Your Embrace.
Ave Maria, Gratia Plena,
Dominus Tecum, Benedicta Tu. [2]

4. As the deer

As the deer panteth for the water
So my soul longeth after Thee
You alone are my heart's desire
And I long to worship Thee
You alone are my strength, my shield
To You alone may my spirit yield
You alone are my heart's desire
And I long to worship Thee
As the deer panteth for the water
So my soul longeth after Thee
You alone are my heart's desire
And I long to worship Thee

You alone are my strength, my shield
To You alone may my spirit yield
You alone are my heart's desire
And I long to worship Thee
You're my friend
And You are my brother
Even though You are a King
I love You more than any other
So much more than anything
You alone are my strength, my shield
To You alone may my spirit yield
You alone are my heart's desire
And I long to worship Thee

5. Away in the manger

Away in a manger
No crib for a bed
The little Lord Jesus
Laid down His sweet head
The stars in the bright sky
Looked down where He lay
The little Lord Jesus
Asleep on the hay
The cattle are lowing
The Baby awakes
But little Lord Jesus
No crying He makes
I love You, Lord Jesus
Look down from the sky
And stay by my side
Until morning is nigh
Be near me, Lord Jesus
I ask You to stay

Close by me forever
And love me I pray
   Bless all the dear children
In Your tender care
And fit us for heaven
To live with You there

6. Be with us Mary

   No Man Can Live As An Island,
Journeying Through Life Alone.
Since We're Most Loved By A Mother,
Jesus Gave Us His Own.
   Be With Us Mary Along The Way,
Guide Every Step We Take.
Lead Us To Jesus Your Loving Son
Come With Us, Mary Come.
   When Jesus Met With Rejection,
Mary Stood By The Cross;
How Can A Mother Desert Her Son?
She'll Also Stand By Us.
   Help Us, Oh Star Of The Ocean,
Be With Us In Our Strife,
When We Are Faced With Temptation,
Tossed By The Storms Of Life.
   Often Enough In Life's Banquet
We Shall Run Short Of Wine.
Then As At Cana, Request Your Son
To Make Our Lives Divine.

7. Blest are you Lord

   Blessed Are You, Lord God Of All Creation.
Through Your Goodness, We Have This Bread To Offer You,
Which Earth Has Given And Human Hands Have Made.

It Will Become For Us The Bread Of Life.
   Blessed Be God For Evermore. (3)
   Blessed Are You, Lord God Of All Creation.
Through Your Goodness, We Have This Wine To Offer You:
Fruit Of The Vine, And The Work Of Human Hands.
It Will Become For Us Our Drink Divine.

8. Carry your candle

   There is a candle in every soul
Some brightly burning, some dark and cold
There is a Spirit who brings fire
Ignites a candle and makes His home
   Chorus
Carry your candle, run to the darkness
Seek out the hopeless, confused and torn
Hold out your candle for all to see it
Take your candle, and go light your world
Take your candle, and go light your world

Frustrated brother, see how he's tried to
Light his own candle some other way
See now your sister, she's been robbed and lied to
Still holds a candle without a flame

We are a family whose hearts are blazing
So let's raise our candles and light up the sky
Praying to our Father, in the name of Jesus
Make us a beacon in darkest times

9. Change my heart

   Change my heart Oh God, make it ever true.
Change my heart Oh God, may I be like You.

    Change my heart Oh God, make it ever true.
Change my heart Oh God, may I be like You.
You are the potter, I am the clay,
Mold me and make me, this is what I pray.
Change my heart Oh God, make it ever true.
Change my heart Oh God, may I be like You.

10. Clap your Hands
    Clap your hands and sing "Hallelujah"!
Reach up to the sky.
Clap your hands and sing "Hallelujah"!
Lift your voices high.
Won't you join the celebration?
Come and let your song ring loud and clear.
Clap your hands and sing "Hallelujah",
'cause a brand new day is here.

You can find a littlebit of sunshine,
even on the darkest day,
and if you try you can chase your troubles away!
So before another day is over,
try your hand at something new
'cause you never know
what's out there waiting for you.

Clap your hands and sing "Hallelujah"!
Reach up to the sky.
Clap your hands and sing "Hallelujah"!
Lift your voices high.
Won't you join the celebration?
Come and let your song ring loud and clear.
Clap your hands and sing "Hallelujah",
'cause a brand new day is here.

Bridge:
Can't you hear us singing,
"Halleluja", "Halleluja", "Halleluja",
"Halleluja", "Halleluja"!

Clap your hands and sing "Hallelujah"!
Reach up to the sky.
Clap your hands and sing "Hallelujah"!
Lift your voices high.
Won't you join the celebration?
Come and let your song ring loud and clear.
Clap your hands and sing "Hallelujah",
'cause a brand new day is here.

11. Come on and celebrate

Come on and celebrate His gift of love,
We will celebrate
The Son of God who loved us
And gave us life.

We'll shout Your praise, O King,
You give us joy nothing else can bring,
We'll give to You our offering
In celebration praise.

Come on and celebrate, celebrate
Celebrate and sing;
Celebrate and sing to the King.

Lift up your voice to praise
The name above ev'ry other name
Jesus the Christ who saved us from sin and death.

Let's bend our knees to Him
Our toungue confess that He's Lord indeed
Let's give to Him our offering in celeration praise

12. Count your Blessings

When upon life's billows you are tempest tossed,
When you are discouraged, thinking all is lost,
Count your many blessings, name them one by one,
And it will surprise you what the Lord hath done.
Refrain:
Count your blessings, name them one by one;
Count your blessings, see what God hath done;
Count your blessings, name them one by one;
Count your many blessings, see what God hath done.
Are you ever burdened with a load of care?
Does the cross seem heavy you are called to bear?
Count your many blessings, ev'ry doubt will fly,
And you will be singing as the days go by. [Refrain]
When you look at others with their lands and gold,
Think that Christ has promised you His wealth untold;
Count your many blessings, money cannot buy
Your reward in heaven, nor your home on high. [Refrain]
So, amid the conflict, whether great or small,
Do not be discouraged, God is over all;
Count your many blessings, angels will attend,
Help and comfort give you to your journey's end. [Refrain]

13. Deck the halls

Deck the halls with boughs of holly, Fa la la la la la la la!

'Tis the season to be jolly, Fa la la la la la la la!
Don we now our gay apparel, Fa la la la la la la la!
Troll the ancient Yuletide carol, Fa la la la la la la la!

See the blazing yule before us, Fa la la la la la la la la!
Strike the harp and join the chorus, Fa la la la la la la la la!

Follow me in merry measure, Fa la la la la la la la la!
While I tell of Yuletide treasure, Fa la la la la la la la la!

Fast away the old year passes, Fa la la la la la la la la!
Hail the new, ye lads and lasses, Fa la la la la la la la la!
Sing we joyous all together! Fa la la la la la la la la!
Heedless of the wind and weather, Fa la la la la la la la la!

14. Enter Rejoice

Enter, rejoice, and come in. Enter, rejoice, and come in.
Today will be a joyful day; enter, rejoice, and come in.
Open your ears to the song. Open your ears to the song.
Today will be a joyful day; enter, rejoice, and come in.
Open your hearts ev'ryone. Open your hearts ev'ryone.
Today will be a joyful day; enter, rejoice, and come in.
Don't be afraid of some change. Don't be afraid of some
change. Today will be a joyful day; enter, rejoice, and come
in.
Enter, rejoice, and come in. Enter, rejoice, and come in.
Today will be a joyful day; enter, rejoice, and come in.

15. Father I place into your hands

Father, I place into Your hands,
The things I cannot do.
Father, I place into Your hands
The times that I've been through.
Father, I place into Your hands
The way that I should go,
For I know I always can trust You.

Father, I place into Your hands
My friends and family.
Father, I place into Your hands
The things that trouble me.
Father, I place into Your hands
The person I would be,
For I know I always can trust You.

Father, we love to see Your face,
Find more lyrics at ※ Mojim.com
We love to hear Your voice.
Father, we love to sing Your praise
And in Your name rejoice.
Father, we love to walk with You
And in Your presence rest,
For we know we always can trust You.

Father, I want to be with You
And do the things You do.
Father, I want to speak the words
That You are speaking too.
Father, I want to love the ones
That You will draw to You,
For I know that I am one with You.

16. Give me oil in my lamp

Give me oil in my lamp, keep me burning.
Give me oil in my lamp, I pray.
Give me oil in my lamp, keep me burning.
Keep me burning till the break of day.
    Refrain:
Sing hosanna, sing hosanna,

sing hosanna to the King of kings!
Sing hosanna, sing hosanna,
sing hosanna to the King!
    Give me love in my heart, keep me sharing.
Give me love in my heart, I pray.
Give me love in my heart, keep me sharing.
Keep me sharing till the break of day. (Refrain)
    Give me joy in my heart, keep me singing.
Give me joy in my heart, I pray.
Give me joy in my heart, keep me singing.
Keep me singing till the break of day. (Refrain)
    Give me faith in my heart, keep me praying.
Give me faith in my heart, I pray.
Give me faith in my heart, keep me praying.
Keep me praying till the break of day. (Refrain)

17. Give thanks to the Lord

    O give thanks to the Lord, for he is good (3)
Yes, eternal is his love.
    I will sing to my God never ceasing,
all my life, I will tell of his wonders:
He's the maker of all earth and heaven,
of the ocean, the seas and all they hold.
    The Almighty is faithful for ever:
He is just to the poor and the outraged:
It is He who gives bread to the hungry
Who delivers the captives from their chains.
    He gives sight to the blind in his mercy;
and he raises the lowly, the humble.
It is he Who gives shelter to strangers,
Every orphan and widow he defends.
    To the just he is gracious and loving.
But the wicked he foils and they stumble.

Yes, the Lord reigns for ever and ever,
He is king over Sion without end.

18. Give Thanks

Give thanks with a grateful heart
Give thanks to the Holy One
Give thanks because He's given Jesus Christ, His Son
Give thanks with a grateful heart
Give thanks to the Holy One
Give thanks because He's given Jesus Christ, His Son
And now let the weak say, "I am strong"
Let the poor say, "I am rich
Because of what the Lord has done for us"
And now let the weak say, "I am strong"
Let the poor say, "I am rich
Because of what the Lord has done for us"

19. Go tell it on the mountains

Go, tell it on the mountain
Over the hills and everywhere
Go, tell it on the mountain
That Jesus Christ is born
While shepherds kept their watching
O'er silent flocks by night
Behold throughout the heavens
There shone a Holy light
Go, tell it on the mountain
Over the hills and everywhere
Go, tell it on the mountain
That Jesus Christ is born
The shepherds feared and trembled
When, lo! Above the Earth
Rang out the angel chorus

That hailed our Savior's birth
    Go, tell it on the mountain
Over the hills and everywhere
Go, tell it on the mountain
That Jesus Christ is born
    Down in a lowly manger
Our humble Christ was born
And brought us all salvation
That blessed Christmas morn
    Go, tell it on the mountain
Over the hills and everywhere
Go, tell it on the mountain
That Jesus Christ is born
That Jesus Christ is born

20. God is dwelling in my heart

    God is dwelling in my heart (2)
He and I are one (2)
All the joy he gives to me (2)
Through Christ his son (2)
And with Jesus in my heart (2)
What have I to fear (2)
For he is the son of God (2)
In my heart he is near

Christians who are baptized
Have you ever realized
The great mystery
God dwells in you and me

This joy God gave to you

Share it then with others too
Show them that God is Love
Lift their hearts above

21. God is good
God is good all the time
He put a song of praise in this heart of mine
God is good all the time
Through the darkest night, His light will shine
God is good, God is good all the time

God is good all the time
He put a song of praise in this heart of mine
God is good all the time
Through the darkest night, His light will shine
God is good, God is good all the time

If you're walking through the valley
And there are shadows all around
Do not fear, He will guide you

He will keep you safe and sound
He has promised to never leave you
Nor forsake you, and His word is true

God is good all the time
He put a song of praise in the heart of mine
God is good all the time
Through the darkest night, His light will shine
God is good, God is good all the time

We were sinners and so unworthy
Still for us He chose to die

Filled us with His Holy Spirit

Now we can stand and testify
That His love is everlasting
And His mercies, they will never end

God is good all the time
He put a song of praise in this heart of mine
God is good all the time
Through the darkest night, His light will shine
God is good, God is good all the time

Though I may not understand
All the plans you have for me
My life is in your hands
And through the eyes of faith
I can clearly see

God is good all the time
He put a song of praise in this heart of mine
God is good all the time
Through the darkest night, His light will shine
God is good, God is good all the time

God is good all the time
He put a song of praise in the heart of mine
God is good all the time
Through the darkest night, His light will shine
God is good, God is good all the time

22. God of mercy and compassion

God of mercy and compassion,
Look with pity upon me,

Father let me call Thee Father,
'Tis thy child returns to Thee.

Jesus Lord, I ask for mercy;
Let me not implore in vain;
All my sins, I now detest them,
Never will I sin again.

By my sins I have deserved
Death and endless misery,
Hell with all its pains and torments,
And for all eternity.

Jesus Lord, I ask for mercy;
Let me not implore in vain;
All my sins, I now detest them,
Never will I sin again.

By my sins I have abandoned
Right and claim to heaven above,
Where the Saints rejoice forever
In a boundless sea of love.

Jesus Lord, I ask for mercy;
Let me not implore in vain;
All my sins, I now detest them,
Never will I sin again.

See our Saviour, bleeding, dying,
On the cross of Calvary;
To that cross my sins have nailed Him,
Yet He bleeds and dies for me.

Jesus Lord, I ask for mercy;
Let me not implore in vain;
All my sins, I now detest them,
Never will I sin again.

23. God still Loves the World
Every tiny star that twinkles in the night sky
Every drop of morning dew
Every spark of fire blazing in the furnace
Every captivating view
Every rainbow in the sky every pretty butterfly

Tells the fascinating news to those who dare to hope...
And the message is God still loves the world, God still, still
loves the world
So throw your life into his hands
Day by day discern his plans
God is passionately busy loving you and me
Every ocean wave that breaks upon the seashore
Every stalk of golden wheat
Every silver stream that gushes down the mountains
Ever drop of honey sweet
Every eagle flying high
Every worm that wriggles by
Tells the fascinating news to those who dare to hope...
And the message is God still loves the world, God still, still
loves the world
So throw your life into his hands
Day by day discern his plans
God is passionately busy loving you and me

Every man & woman pledge in love forever
Every little new born child

Ever voice of favor of a needy neighbor
Every radiating smile
Every hand that offers love
Every furring flow of blood
Tells the fascinating news to those who dare to hope...
And the message is God still loves the world, God still, still
loves the world

So throw your life into his hands
Day by day discern his plans
God is passionately busy loving you and me
God is passionately busy loving you and me
God is passionately busy loving you and me.

24. God's love is so wonderful
    God's love it's so wonderful
God's love it's so wonderful
God's love it's so wonderful
Oh! Wonderful love!
    So high you can't get over it
So high you can't get over it
So high you can't get over it
Oh! Wonderful love!
    So deep you can't get under it
So deep you can't get under it
So deep you can't get under it
Oh! Wonderful love!
    So wide you can't get around it
So wide you can't get around it
So wide you can't get around it
Oh! Wonderful love!
    God's love it's so wonderful
God's love it's so wonderful

God's love it's so wonderful
Oh! Wonderful love!

25. Great and mighty

Great and mighty is the Lord our God;
Great and mighty is He.
Great and mighty is the Lord our God;
Great and mighty is He.
Lift His banner, let the anthem ring
Praises to our mighty King.
Great and mighty is the Lord our God;
Great and mighty is He.
Sing to Jesus with a song of praise;
Sing to Jesus with praise.
Sing to Jesus with a song of praise;
Sing to Jesus with praise.
Fill the heavens with a mighty voice;
Bless His name, let all rejoice.
Sing to Jesus with a song of praise;
Sing to Jesus with praise.

26. Great indeed are your works

Great indeed are your works O lord now and evermore
Great indeed are your works O lord now and evermore
The universe night and day
Tells of all your wonders
You are our life and our light
We shall praise you always
Great indeed are your works O lord now and evermore
Great indeed are your works O lord now and evermore
Great indeed are your works O lord now and evermore
Great indeed are your works O lord now and evermore
You are the path which we tread you will lead us onward

From every corner of the Earth
All the nations gather
Great indeed are your works O lord now and evermore
Great indeed are your works O lord now and evermore

27. Here I am to worship

Light of the world, You stepped down into darkness
Opened my eyes, let me see
Beauty that made this heart adore You
Hope of a life spent with You

Here I am to worship, here I am to bow down
Here I am to say that You're my God
You're altogether lovely, altogether worthy
Altogether wonderful to me

King of all days, oh so highly exalted
Glorious in Heaven above
Humbly You came to the earth You created
All for love's sake became poor

Here I am to worship, here I am to bow down
Here I am to say that You're my God
You're altogether lovely, altogether worthy
Altogether wonderful to me

Here I am to worship, here I am to bow down
Here I am to say that You're my God
You're altogether lovely, altogether worthy
Altogether wonderful to me
Find more lyrics at ※ Mojim.com

Never know how much it cost to see my sin upon that cross

Never know how much it cost to see my sin upon that cross
I'll never know how much it cost to see my sin upon that
cross

Here I am to worship, here I am to bow down
Here I am to say that You're my God
You're altogether lovely, altogether worthy
Altogether wonderful to me

Here I am to worship, here I am to bow down
Here I am to say that You're my God
You're altogether lovely, altogether worthy
Altogether wonderful to me

Here I am to worship, here I am to bow down
Here I am to say that You're my God
You're altogether lovely, altogether worthy
Altogether wonderful to me

Here I am to worship, here I am to bow down
Here I am to say that You're my God
You're altogether lovely, altogether worthy
Altogether wonderful to me

28. Here we are

here we are
Lifting our hands to You
Here we are
Giving You thanks for all You do
And as we praise
And worship Your holy name
You are here
Dwelling within our praise

For every answered prayer
Oh yeah, for always being there
For love that hears us when we call
For arms that lift us when we fall, oh Lord
Oh, You have always been
Right beside us, leading us all along the way
And we made it through (we made it through)
Because of You
And here we are
Lifting our hands to You
Here we are
Giving You thanks for all You do
And as we praise
And worship Your holy name
You are here, yes You are
Dwelling within our praise
For days we cannot see (for days we cannot see)
For all that yet to be (so much is yet to be)
The trials we may have to face
When we'll be leaning on your grace, oh yes
It will be your strength, yes it will
That saves us
Your love that makes us strong
And through it all (through it all)
We'll sing this song, oh
Here we are
Lifting our hands to You, worshipping
Here we are
Giving You thanks for all You do (oh, thank you)
As we praise
And worship Your holy name
You are here, yes You are
Dwelling within our praise (yes, thank God)

You are here
Dwelling within our praise (oh, we thank You, Lord)
You are here
Dwelling within our praise (yes, you are)
    Oh, we thank You, Lord (thank You)
We thank You, Lord (thank You)
You inhabit the praises of Your people
So you're here with us right now
We thank You, we thank You
For Your presence, we praise You

29. Here we are

Here we are all together as we sing a song our song joyfully;
Here we are joined together, as we pray we'll always be.

Join we now as friends
And celebrate the unity we share, all as one
Keep the fire burning, kindle it with care
And we'll all join in & sing chorus

Let us make this world an alleluia,
Let us make this world a better place
Keep a smile handy, lend a helping hand
And we'll all join in & sing chorus

Glorify our God with all our voices
Show him we are sincere by all our deeds
Shout the joys of freedom everywhere
Let us all join in and sing. chorus

30. Hide me now

Hide me now
Under Your wings

Cover me
Within Your mighty hand

When the oceans rise and thunders roar
I will soar with you above the storm
Father, You are King over the flood
I will be still and know You are God

Hide me now
Under Your wings
Cover me
Within Your mighty hand

When the oceans rise and thunders roar
I will soar with you above the storm
Father, You are King over the flood
Find more lyrics at ✕ Mojim.com
I will be still and know You are God

Find rest my soul
In Christ alone
Know His power
In quietness and trust

When the oceans rise and thunders roar
I will soar with you above the storm
Father, You are King over the flood
I will be still and know You are God

When the oceans rise and thunders roar
I will soar with you above the storm
Father, You are King over the flood
I will be still and know You are God

31. Holy, Holy, Holy Lord

Holy, holy, holy Lord,
God of power and might,
heaven and earth are full of your glory.
Hosanna in the highest.
Hosanna! Hosanna! Hosanna in the highest.
Blessed is he who comes in the name,
who comes in the name of the Lord.
Blessed is he! Blessed is he
who comes in the name of the Lord.
Holy, holy, holy Lord,
God of power and might,
heaven and earth are full of your glory.
Hosanna in the highest.
Hosanna! Hosanna! Hosanna in the highest.

32. Hosanna in the highest

Lord, we lift up your name, with our hearts full of praise,
Be exalted, O Lord, my God,
Hosanna in the highest!

Glory, glory, glory to the King of kings! (2X)
Lord, we lift up your name, with our hearts full of praise,
Be exalted, O Lord our God,
Hosanna in the highest!

Jesus, Jesus, Jesus, to the King of kings! (2X)
Lord, we lift up your name, with our hearts full of praise,
Be exalted, O Lord our God,
Hosanna in the highest

33. How great thou art

O Lord my God, when I in awesome wonder
Consider all the works Thy hands have made,
I see the stars, I hear the rolling thunder,
Thy pow'r thru-out the universe displayed!
    Chorus
Then sings my soul, my Savior God, to Thee;
How great Thou art, how great Thou art!
Then sings my soul, my Savior God, to Thee;
How great Thou art, how great Thou art!

When thru the woods and forest glades I wander
And hear the birds sing sweetly in the trees,
When I look down from lofty mountain grandeur
And hear the brook and feel the gentle breeze,

And when I think that God, His Son not sparing,
Sent Him to die, I scarce can take it in –
That on the cross, my burden gladly bearing,
He bled and died to take away my sin!

When Christ shall come with shout of acclamation
And take me home, what joy shall fill my heart!
Then I shall bow in humble adoration
And there proclaim, my God, how great Thou art!

34. I have decided to follow Jesus
    I have decided to follow Jesus;
I have decided to follow Jesus;
I have decided to follow Jesus;
No turning back, no turning back.
    Tho' none go with me, I still will follow,
Tho' none go with me I still will follow,
Tho' none go with me, I still will follow;

No turning back, no turning back.
    My cross I'll carry, till I see Jesus;
My cross I'll carry till I see Jesus,
My cross I'll carry till I see Jesus;
No turning back, No turning back.
    The world behind me, the cross before me,
The world behind me, the cross before me;
The world behind me, the cross before me;
No turning back, no turning back.

35. I offer my life

    Lord, I offer my life to You
Everything I've been through
Use it for Your glory
Lord I offer my days to You
Lifting my praise to You
As a pleasing sacrifice
Lord I offer You my life
    Things in the past
Things in the past
Things yet unseen
Wishes and dreams that are yet to come true
All of my hopes
And all of my planes
My heart and my hands are lifted to You
    Lord, I offer my life to You
Everything I've been through
Use it for Your glory
Lord I offer my days to You
Lifting my praise to You
As a pleasing sacrifice
Lord I offer You my life

And Lord, I offer my life to You
Everything I've been through
Use it for Your glory
Lord I offer my days to You
Lifting my praise to You
As a pleasing sacrifice
Lord I offer You my life

36. I will sing of the mercies

I will sing of the mercies of the Lord forever,
I will sing, I will sing,
I will sing of the mercies of the Lord forever,
I will sing of the mercies of the Lord.
With my mouth will I make known
Thy faithfulness, Thy faithfulness,
With my mouth will I make known
Thy faithfulness to all generations,
I will sing of the mercies of the Lord forever,
I will sing of the mercies of the Lord.

37. Immaculate Mary

Immaculate Mary, your praises we sing.
You reign now in Heaven with Jesus our King.

Ave, Ave, Ave, Maria! Ave, Ave, Ave, Maria!

In Heaven the blessed your glory proclaim;
On earth we your children invoke your sweet name.

Ave, Ave, Ave, Maria! Ave, Ave, Ave, Maria!

We pray for our Mother, the Church upon earth,
And bless, Holy Mary, the land of our birth.

Ave, Ave, Ave, Maria! Ave, Ave, Ave, Maria!

38. In his time

In his time, in his time
He makes all things beautiful
In his time
Lord please show me everyday
As you're teaching me your way
That you do just what you say
In your time
In your time, in your time
You make all things beautiful
In your time
Lord my life to you I bring
May each song I have to sing
Be to you a lovely thing
In your time
Lord please show me everyday
As you teaching me your way
That you do just what you say
In your time
In your time (in your time), in your time (in your time
lord)
You make all things beautiful
In your time (in your time)
Lord my life to you I bring
May each song I have to sing
Be to you a lovely thing
In your time
Be to you a lovely thing
In your time

39. In the name of Jesus

In the name of Jesus, in the name of Jesus,
we have the victory.
In the name of Jesus, in the name of Jesus,
Satan, you have to flee.
Oh, what can ever stand before us
when we call on that great name?
Jesus, Jesus, precious Jesus,
we have the victory.
In the name of Jesus, in the name of Jesus,
we have the victory.
In the name of Jesus, in the name of Jesus,
Satan, you have to flee.
Oh, Tell me, who can stand before us
when we call on that great name?
Jesus, Jesus, precious Jesus,
we have the victory.
Optional chorus:
Victory, oh, victory,
we have the victory.
Victory, oh, victory,
we have the victory.

40. Jingle bell

Dashing through the snow
On a one horse open sleigh
O'er the fields we go,
Laughing all the way
Bells on bob tail ring,
making spirits bright
What fun it is to laugh and sing
A sleighing song tonight

Oh, jingle bells, jingle bells
Jingle all the way
Oh, what fun it is to ride
In a one horse open sleigh
Jingle bells, jingle bells
Jingle all the way
Oh, what fun it is to ride
In a one horse open sleigh

A day or two ago,
I thought I'd take a ride,
And soon Miss Fanny Bright
Was seated by my side;
The horse was lean and lank
Misfortune seemed his lot
We got into a drifted bank,
And then we got upsot.

Oh, jingle bells, jingle bells
Jingle all the way
Oh, what fun it is to ride
In a one horse open sleigh
Jingle bells, jingle bells
Jingle all the way
Oh, what fun it is to ride
In a one horse open sleigh

Jingle Bells, Jingle Bells,
Jingle all the way!
Oh, What fun it is to ride
In a one horse open sleigh.
Jingle Bells, Jingle Bells,

Jingle all the way!
Oh, What fun it is to ride
In a one horse open sleigh.

Now the ground is white
Go it while you're young
Take the girls tonight
And sing this sleighing song
Just get a bob tailed bay
two-forty as his speed
Hitch him to an open sleigh
And crack! you'll take the lead

Jingle Bells, Jingle Bells,
Jingle all the way!
Oh, What fun it is to ride
In a one horse open sleigh.
Jingle Bells, Jingle Bells,
Jingle all the way!
Oh, What fun it is to ride
In a one horse open sleigh.

41. Jingle bell rock

Jingle bell, jingle bell, jingle bell rock
Jingle bells swing and jingle bells ring
Snowin' and blowin' up bushels of fun
Now the jingle hop has begun
Jingle bell, jingle bell, jingle bell rock
Jingle bells chime in jingle bell time
Dancin' and prancin' in Jingle Bell Square
In the frosty air
What a bright time, it's the right time
To rock the night away

Jingle bell time is a swell time
To go glidin' in a one-horse sleigh
     Giddy-up jingle horse, pick up your feet
Jingle around the clock
Mix and a-mingle in the jinglin' feet
That's the jingle bell rock
     Jingle bell, jingle bell, jingle bell rock
Jingle bells chime in jingle bell time
Dancin' and prancin' in Jingle Bell Square
In the frosty air
     What a bright time, it's the right time
To rock the night away
Jingle bell time is a swell time
To go glidin' in a one-horse sleigh
     Giddy-up jingle horse, pick up your feet
Jingle around the clock
Mix and a-mingle in the jinglin' feet
That's the jingle bell
That's the jingle bell
That's the jingle bell rock

42. Joy to the world

     Joy to the world, the Lord is come
Let earth receive her King
Let every heart prepare Him room
And heaven and nature sing
And heaven and nature sing
And heaven, and heaven and nature sing
     Joy to the world, the Savior reigns
Let all their songs employ
While fields and floods
Rocks, hills and plains
Repeat the sounding joy

Repeat the sounding joy
Repeat, repeat the sounding joy
Here we go
    Joy, unspeakable joy
An overflowing well
No tongue can tell
Joy, unspeakable joy
It rises in my soul
Never lets me go
    He rules the world, with truth and grace
And makes the nations prove
The glories of His righteousness
And wonders of His love
And wonders of His love
And wonders, wonders of His love
Joy!
    Joy, unspeakable joy
An overflowing well
No tongue can tell
Joy, unspeakable joy
It rises in my soul
Never lets me go

43. Jumbo, Jesus loves you
    Jumbo !
Jesus loves you
Are you happy?
HE is with you
Kareebo into HIS presence
Why do you worry
Hakuna-matata
    ohhh ohhh ohhh !
Almighty GOD.

44. Just like a child

Just like a child who trusts his father dear And who delights to feel his presence near
Just like a child whose mind has not a doubt.
And whose heart is never proud.

Ch. Here I come, O Lord,
Here I come, just like a child.
Here I come, O Lord,
Here I come just like a child.

Just like a child so weak he cannot stand, But who holds firm and tight his mother's hand,
Just like a child who sings in bright daylight, Fearing not the long dark night.

Just like a Child that guitly deeds oppress With mind and heart in trouble and distress, Who throws himself into his mother's arms,
Sure she'll free him form his qualms.

45. Kyrie elesion

Kyrie eleison, .Lord, have mercy.
Kyrie eleison. Lord, have mercy.
Christe eleison, Christ, have mercy.
Christe eleison. Christ, have mercy.
Kyrie eleison Lord, have mercy.
Kyrie eleison. Lord, have mercy.

46. Listen

Listen! let your heart keep seeking,
Listen to His constant speaking,
Listen to the Spirit calling you.
Listen to His inspiration,
Listen to His invitation,

Listen to the Spirit calling you.

He's in the sound of the thunder, in the whisper of the breeze.

He's in the might of the whirlwind in the roaring of the seas.

Listen! let your heart keep seeking,
Listen to His constant speaking,
Listen to the Spirit calling you.

47. Living waters

Living waters flow on
Sweep away my pain
Bring your healing to my heart
Help me love once again
Cares and worries let me down
Fear of failure fills my day
When I'm lost and all alone
Help me Lord to find my way.
Am People knocking at my door,
Strangers seeking love and care
Never let me turn them down,
Show me gently how to share.

48. Lord have mercy

Lord, have mercy on your people gathered here
Christ, have mercy on your people gathered here
We confess we have sinned
In thought and word and deed
Lord, have mercy on your people gathered here.

49. Lord I lift your name on high

Lord I lift Your name on high
Lord I love to sing Your praises

I'm so glad You're in my life
I'm so glad You came to save us
    You came from heaven to earth to show the way
From the earth to the cross, my debt to pay
From the cross to the grave, from the grave to the sky
Lord I lift Your name on high
    Lord I lift Your name on high
Lord I love to sing Your praises
I'm so glad You're in my life
I'm so glad You came to save us
    You came from heaven to earth to show the way
From the earth to the cross, my debt to pay
From the cross to the grave, from the grave to the sky
Lord I lift Your name on high
    You came from heaven to earth to show the way
From the earth to the cross, my debt to pay
From the cross to the grave, from the grave to the sky
Lord I lift Your name on high
    You came from heaven to earth to show the way
From the earth to the cross, my debt to pay
From the cross to the grave, from the grave to the sky
Lord I lift Your name on high

50. Make me a channel

    Make me a channel of your peace
Where there is hatred let me bring your love
Where there is injury, your pardon Lord
And where there is doubt true faith in You
    Make me a channel of your peace
Where there is despair in life let me bring hope
Where there is darkness only light
And where there's sadness ever joy

Oh, Master grant that I may never seek
So much to be consoled as to console
To be understood as to understand
To be loved as to love with all my soul
   Make me a channel of your peace
It is in pardoning that we are pardoned
It is in giving to all men that we receive
And in dying that we are born to eternal life
   Oh, Master grant that I may never seek
So much to be consoled as to console
To be understood as to understand
To be loved as to love with all my soul
   Make me a channel of your peace
Where there's despair in life let me bring hope
Where there is darkness only light
And where there's sadness ever joy

51. Making melody

   Making Melody In My Heart (3)
Unto The King Of Kings.
   Making Melody In My Heart (3)
Unto The King Of Kings.
   Now Thumbs In
Making Melody In My Heart (3)
Unto The King Of Kings.
   So Thumbs In, Elbows Out
Making Melody In My Heart (3)
Unto The King Of Kings.
   Thumbs In, Elbows Out, Knees Bend
Making Melody In My Heart (3)
Unto The King Of Kings.
   So Thumbs In, Elbows Out, Knees Bend, Feet Apart
Making Melody In My Heart (3)

Unto The King Of Kings.
Thumbs In, Elbows Out, Knees Bend, Feet Apart, Turn
Around
Making Melody In My Heart (3)
Unto The King Of Kings.
So Thumbs In, Elbows Out, Knees Bend,
Feet Apart, Turn Around, Tongues Out
Making Melody In My Heart (3)
Unto The King Of Kings.

52. Mary's boy child

Mary's boy child Jesus Christ was born on Christmas
Day
And man will live for evermore because of Christmas Day
Long time ago in Bethlehem, so the Holy Bible said
Mary's boy child Jesus Christ was born on Christmas Day
Hark, now hear the angels sing, a king was born today
And man will live for evermore, because of Christmas Day
Mary's boy child Jesus Christ was born on Christmas Day
While shepherds watch their flocks by night
They see a bright new shining star
They hear a choir sing a song, the music seemed to come
from afar
Hark, now hear the angels sing, a king was born today
And man will live for evermore, because of Christmas Day
For a moment the world was aglow, all the bells rang out
There were tears of joy and laughter, people shouted
"Let everyone know, there is hope for all to find peace"

53. More love, More power

More love, more power
More of You in my life
More love, more power

More of You in my life
    And I will worship You, with all of my heart
I will worship You, with all of my mind
I will worship You, with all of my strength
For You are my Lord
    More love, more power
More of You in my life
More love, more power
More of You in my life
    And I will worship You, with all of my heart
I will worship You, with all of my mind
I will worship You, with all of my strength
For You are my Lord
    More love
    More love, more power
More of You in my life
More love, more power
More of You in my life
    More love, more power
    More love, more power
More of You in my life
More love, more power
More of You in my life
    More love, more power
More of You in my life
More love, more power
More of You in my life
    More love, more power
More of You in my life
More love, more power
More of You in my life
    More love, more power
More of You in my life

More love, more power
More of You in my life

54. Mother of mine

Mother of mine you gave to me, all of my life to do as I please,
I owe everything I have to you,
Mother sweet mother of mine.

Mother of mine when I was young
You showed me the right way things had to be done,
Without your arms where would I be,
Mother sweet mother of mine.

Chorus:
Mother you gave me happiness, much more than words can say,
I thank the Lord that He may bless you, every night and every day.

Mother of mine now I am grown and I can walk straight all on my own,
I'd like to give you what you gave to me,
Mother sweet mother of mine.

Chorus
Mother of mine now I am grown and I can walk straight all on my own,
I'd like to give you what you gave to me,
Mother sweet mother of mine.

55. O come all ye faithful

Oh, come, all ye faithful,

Joyful and triumphant!
Oh, come ye, oh come ye to Bethlehem.
Come and behold him,
Born the King of angels;
[Chorus]
Oh, come, let us adore him;
Oh, come, let us adore him;
Oh, come, let us adore him,
Christ, the Lord.
Sing, choirs of angels,
Sing in exultation;
Sing, all ye citizens of heav'n above!
Glory to God,
Glory in the highest;
Yea, Lord, we greet thee,
Born this happy morning;
Jesus, to thee be all glory giv'n.
Son of the Father,
Now in flesh appearing;

56. Power of your love

Lord, I come to You
Let my heart be changed, renewed
Flowing from the grace
That I found in You
Lord, I've come to know
The weaknesses I see in me
Will be stripped away
By the power of Your love

[Chorus]
Hold me close
Let Your love surround me

Bring me near
Draw me to Your side
And as I wait
I'll rise up like the eagle
And I will soar with You
Your Spirit leads me on
In the power of Your love
    Lord, unveil my eyes
Let me see You face to face
The knowledge of Your love
As You live in me
Lord, renew my mind
As Your will unfolds in my life
In living every day
By the power of Your love

[Chorus]
Hold me close
Let Your love surround me
Bring me near
Draw me to Your side
And as I wait
I'll rise up like the eagle
And I will soar with You
Your Spirit leads me on
In the power of Your love
Hold me close
Let Your love surround me
Bring me near
Draw me to Your side
And as I wait
I'll rise up like the eagle
And I will soar with You

Your Spirit leads me on
In the power of Your love
And I will soar with You
Your Spirit leads me on
In the power of Your love
And I will soar with You
Your Spirit leads me on
In the power of Your love

57. Praise him

Praise him, praise him,
praise him in the morning,
praise him in the noontime.
Praise him, praise him,
praise him when the sun goes down.
Love him, love him,
love him in the morning,
love him in the noontime.
love him, love him,
love him when the sun goes down.
Trust him, trust him,
trust him in the morning,
trust him in the noontime.
Trust him, trust him,
trust him when the sun goes down.
Serve him, serve him,
serve him in the morning,
serve him in the noontime.
Serve him, serve him,
serve him when the sun goes down.
Jesus, Jesus,
Jesus in the morning,
Jesus in the noontime.

Jesus, Jesus,
Jesus when the sun goes down.

58. Rejoice in the Lord, Always

Rejoice in the Lord always and again I say rejoice,
Rejoice in the Lord always and again I say rejoice!
Rejoice, rejoice, and again I say rejoice,
Rejoice, rejoice, and again I say rejoice!
Rejoice in the Lord always and again I say rejoice,
Rejoice in the Lord always and again I say rejoice!
Rejoice, rejoice, and again I say rejoice,
Rejoice, rejoice, and again I say rejoice!

59. Rudolph

Rudolph, the red-nosed reindeer
had a very shiny nose.
And if you ever saw him,
you would even say it glowed.
All of the other reindeer
used to laugh and call him names.
They never let poor Rudolph
join in any reindeer games.
Then one foggy Christmas eve
Santa came to say:
"Rudolph with your nose so bright,
won't you guide my sleigh tonight?"
Then all the reindeer loved him
as they shouted out with glee:
"Rudolph the red-nosed reindeer,
you'll go down in history!"

60. Save us saviour

Save us, Savior of the world,
for by your Cross and Resurrection
you have set us free.

61. Seek yee first

Seek ye first the Kingdom of God
And His righteousness
And all these things shall be added unto you
Allelu Alleluia
Ask and it shall be given unto you
Seek and ye shall find
Knock and it shall be opened unto you
Allelu Alleluia
Al - le - lu - ia
Al - le - lu - ia
Al - le - lu - ia
Al - le - lu Al - le - lu - ia
Al - le - lu - ia
Al - le - lu - ia
Al - le - lu - ia
Al - le - lu Al - le - lu - ia

62. Shepherd of my soul

Shepherd of my soul I give You full control
Wherever You may lead I will follow
I have made the choice to listen for Your voice
Wherever You may lead I will go
Be it in a quiet pasture or by a gentle breeze
The shepherd of my soul is by my side
Should I face a mighty mountain or a valley dark and deep
The shepherd of my soul will be my guide

63. Shine Jesus Shine

Lord, the light of your love is shining
In the midst of the darkness, shining
Jesus, Light of the world, shine upon us
Set us free by the truth you now bring us
Shine on me, shine on me
    Shine, Jesus, shine
Fill this land with the Father's glory
Blaze, Spirit, blaze
Set our hearts on fire
Flow, river, flow
Flood the nations with grace and mercy
Send forth your word
Lord, and let there be light
    Lord, I come to your awesome presence
From the shadows into your radiance
By the blood I may enter your brightness
Search me, try me, consume all my darkness
Shine on me, shine on me
    Shine, Jesus, shine
Fill this land with the Father's glory
Blaze, Spirit, blaze
Set our hearts on fire
Flow, river, flow
Flood the nations with grace and mercy
Send forth your word
Lord, and let there be light
    As we gaze on your kingly brightness
So our faces display your likeness
Ever changing from glory to glory
Mirrored here may our lives tell your story
Shine on me, shine on me
    Shine, Jesus, shine
Fill this land with the Father's glory

Blaze, Spirit, blaze
Set our hearts on fire
Flow, river, flow
Flood the nations with grace and mercy
Send forth your word
Lord, and let there be

64. Shout to the Lord

My Jesus, my Saviour
Lord there is none like You
All of my days I want to praise
The wonders of Your mighty love
My comfort, my shelter
Tower of refuge and strength
Let every breath, all that I am
Never cease to worship You
Shout to the Lord all the Earth, let us sing
Power and majesty, praise to the King
Mountains bow down and the seas will roar
At the sound of Your name
I sing for joy at the work of Your hands
Forever I'll love You, forever I'll stand
Nothing compares to the promise I have
In You

65. Showers of blessing

There shall be showers of blessing:
This is the promise of love;
There shall be seasons refreshing,
Sent from the Savior above.
Showers of blessing,
Showers of blessing we need;
Mercy-drops round us are falling,

But for the showers we plead.
    There shall be showers of blessing—
Precious reviving again;
Over the hills and the valleys,
Sound of abundance of rain.
    There shall be showers of blessing;
Send them upon us, O Lord!
Grant to us now a refreshing;
Come, and now honor Thy Word.
    There shall be showers of blessing;
O that today they might fall,
Now as to God we're confessing,
Now as on Jesus we call!
    There shall be showers of blessing,
If we but trust and obey;
There shall be seasons refreshing,
If we let God have His way.

66. Silent night

    Silent night, holy night!
All is calm, all is bright.
Round yon Virgin, Mother and Child.
Holy infant so tender and mild,
Sleep in heavenly peace,
Sleep in heavenly peace

Silent night, holy night!
Shepherds quake at the sight.
Glories stream from heaven afar
Heavenly hosts sing Alleluia,
Christ the Savior is born!
Christ the Savior is born

Silent night, holy night!
Son of God love's pure light.
Radiant beams from Thy holy face
With dawn of redeeming grace,
Jesus Lord, at Thy birth
Jesus Lord, at Thy birth

67. The gift of God

Every person is a gift of God (3)
A wonderful marvellous gift
I am a gift
You are a gift
A very special gift
Unique in all the world

68. This is the day

This is the day, this is the day.
That the Lord has made, that the Lord has made.
We will rejoice, we will rejoice,
And be glad in it, and be glad in it.
This is the day that the Lord has made.
We will rejoice and be glad in it.
This is the day, this is the day
That the Lord has made.
We are the sons, we are the sons,
Of the living God, of the living God.
We will rejoice, we will rejoice,
And be glad in Him, and be glad in Him.
We are the sons of the living God.
We will rejoice and be glad in Him.
We are the sons, we are the sons
Of the living God.

69. Thy loving Kindness

    Thy lovingkindness is better than life
Thy lovingkindness is better than life
My lips shall praise thee, thus still I bless thee
I will lift up my hands unto thy name
    I lift my hands up unto thy name
I lift my hands up unto thy name
My lips shall praise thee, thus still I bless thee
I will lift up my hands unto thy name

70. Thy word

    Thy Word is a lamp unto my feet and a light unto my path
Thy Word is a lamp unto my feet and a light unto my path
    When I feel afraid
Think I've lost my way
Still you're there right beside me
And nothing will I fear
As long as you are near
Please be near me to the end
    Thy Word is a lamp unto my feet and a light unto my path
Thy Word is a lamp unto my feet and a light unto my path
    I will not forget
Your love for me and yet
My heart forever is wandering
Jesus be my guide
And hold me to your side
I will love you to the end
    Nothing will I fear as long as you are near
Please be near me to the end

Thy Word is a lamp unto my feet and a light unto my
path
Thy Word is a lamp unto my feet and a light unto my path
And a light unto my path
You're the light unto my path

71. Walking in the light of the Lord

It's a great thing to praise the Lord
It's a great thing to praise the Lord
It's a great thing to praise the Lord
Walking in the light of God
Walk, walk, walk, walk in the light
Walk, walk, walk, walk in the light
Walk, walk, walk, walk in the light
Walking in the light of God
It's a great thing to love the Lord
It's a great thing to love the Lord
It's a great thing to love the Lord
Walking in the light of God
Walk, walk, walk, walk in the light
Walk, walk, walk, walk in the light
Walk, walk, walk, walk in the light
Walking in the light of God
It's a great thing to serve the Lord
It's a great thing to serve the Lord
It's a great thing to serve the Lord
Walking in the light of God
Walk, walk, walk, walk in the light
Walk, walk, walk, walk in the light
Walk, walk, walk, walk in the light
Walking in the light of God

72. Walking with the Lord

Walking with the Lord,
We are walking in the morning,
Lift up your hearts,
For you are walking with God.
Singing to the Lord,
We are singing in the sunshine,
Lift up our hearts,
For you are singing to God.
Hand in hand with everyone,
We're walking, walking,
Black and white and brown,
Together, walking, walking,
Singing new songs now,
Living new lives,
Building new bridges,
Walking distant miles,
We' we're walking with the Lord....
Rain and storm will not prevent us,
Walking, walking,
Faith and hope and love,
Will send us walking, walking.
Crossing all barriers,
Climbing all stiles,
Breaking through fences,
Walking distant miles,
Well we're walking the the Lord....

73. We proclaim your death O Lord

We proclaim your death, O Lord, and profess your resurrection until you come again.

74. We shall overcome

We Shall Overcome,

we shall overcome
We shall overcome someday.
Oh, deep in my heart,
I do believe, We shall overcome someday.
We are not afraid,
we are not afraid,
We are not afraid today.
Oh, deep in my heart,
I do believe, We shall overcome someday.
We are not alone,
we are not alone
We are not alone today
Oh, deep in my heart,
I do believe, We are not alone today.
The truth will make us free,
the truth will make us free,
The truth will make us free someday.
Oh, deep in my heart,
I do believe, We shall overcome someday.
We'll walk hand in hand,
we'll walk hand in hand,
We'll walk hand in hand someday.
Oh, deep in my heart,
I do believe, We shall overcome someday.
The Lord will see us through,
the Lord will see us through,
The Lord will see us through someday.
Oh, deep in my heart,
I do believe, We shall overcome someday.
Black and white together,
Black and white together,
Black and white together someday.
Oh, deep in my heart,

I do believe, We shall overcome someday.
We shall all be free,
we shall all be free,
We shall all be free someday.
Oh, deep in my heart,
I do believe, We shall overcome someday.

75. What a friend we have.

What a friend we have in Jesus
All our sins and griefs to bear
What a privilege to carry
Everything to God in prayer
Oh, what peace we often forfeit
Oh, what needless pain we bear
All because we do not carry
Everything to God in prayer
Have we trials and temptations?
Is there trouble anywhere?
We should never be discouraged
Take it to the Lord in prayer
Can we find a friend so faithful
Who will all our sorrows share?
Jesus knows our every weakness
Take it to the Lord in prayer

76. Whatsoever you do

Whatsover you do to the least of my brothers
That you do unto me.
Whatsoever you do to the least of my sisters
That you do unto me.
When I was hungry, you gave me to eat;
When I was thirsty you gave me to drink.
Now enter into the home of my Father.

When I was weary, you helped me find rest;
When I was anxious, you calmed all my fears.
Now enter into the home of my Father.
When I was homeless, you opened your door;
When I was naked, you gave me your coat.
Now enter into the home of my Father.
When in a prison, you came to my cell;
When on a sickbed, you cared for my needs.
Now enter into the home of my Father.
When I was laughed at, you stood by my side;
When I was happy, you shared in my joy.
Now enter into the home of my Father.

77. **When we eat**

When we eat this Bread,
And drink this cup,
We proclaim your Death, O Lord,

Until you come again,
Until you come again
We proclaim your death, O Lord

78. **You raise me up**

When I am down and, oh my soul, so weary
When troubles come and my heart burdened be
Then, I am still and wait here in the silence
Until You come and sit awhile with me.
You raise me up, so I can stand on mountains
You raise me up, to walk on stormy seas
I am strong, when I am on your shoulders
You raise me up to more than I can be
You raise me up, so I can stand on mountains
You raise me up, to walk on stormy seas

I am strong, when I am on your shoulders
You raise me up to more than I can be.
    You raise me up, so I can stand on mountains
You raise me up, to walk on stormy seas
I am strong, when I am on your shoulders
You raise me up to more than I can be.
    You raise me up, so I can stand on mountains
You raise me up, to walk on stormy seas
I am strong, when I am on your shoulders
You raise me up to more than I can be.
    You raise me up to more than I can be.

Prayers

As a part of one's daily walk with God the Prayer Book becomes a beloved companion, an aid to understanding and worship, a mentor in prayer and meditation, and, in effect, a cherished spiritual director.

4

Common Prayers

Sign Of The Cross

In the name of the Father, and of the Son, and of the Holy Spirit.

1. Morning Prayer

Come Holy Spirit, fill the hearts of Thy faithful, and kindle in them the fire of Thy love.

Most holy and adorable Trinity, one God in three Persons, I believe that Thou art here present; I adore Thee with the deepest humility, and render to Thee, with my whole heart, the homage which is due to Thy sovereign majesty.

O my God, I most humbly thank Thee for all the favors Thou hast bestowed upon me up to the present moment. I give Thee thanks from the bottom of my heart that Thou hast created me after Thine own image and likeness, that Thou hast redeemed me by the precious blood of Thy dear Son, and that Thou hast preserved me and brought me safe to the beginning of another day. I offer to Thee, O Lord, my whole being, and in particular all my thoughts, words, actions, and sufferings of this day. I consecrate them all to the glory of Thy name, beseeching Thee that through the infinite merits of Jesus Christ my Saviour they may all find acceptance in Thy sight. May Thy divine love animate them, and may they all tend to Thy greater glory.

Adorable Jesus, my Saviour and Master, model of all perfection, I resolve and will endeavor this day to imitate Thy example, to be, like Thee, mild, humble, chaste, zealous, charitable, and resigned. I will redouble my efforts that I may not fall this day into any of those sins which I have heretofore committed (here you may name any besetting sin), and which I sincerely desire to forsake.

O my God, Thou knowest my poverty and weakness, and that I am unable to do anything good without Thee; deny me not, O God, the help of Thy grace; proportion it to my necessities; give me strength to avoid everything evil which Thou forbiddest, and to practice the good which Thou hast commanded; and enable me to bear patiently all the trials which it may please Thee to send me.
Amen.

2. Our Father

Our Father, who art in heaven, hallowed be
thy name. Thy kingdom come, thy will be done,
on earth, as it is in heaven. Give us this day our
daily bread and forgive us our trespasses as we
forgive those who trespass against us; and lead us
not into temptation, but deliver us from evil.
Amen.

3. Hail Mary

Hail Mary,
Full of Grace,
The Lord is with thee.
Blessed art thou among women,
and blessed is the fruit
of thy womb, Jesus.

Holy Mary,
Mother of God,
pray for us sinners now,
and at the hour of our death.

4. Glory be

Glory be to the Father,
and to the Son,
and to the Holy Spirit.
As it was in the beginning, is now,
and ever shall be,
world without end.

5. Apostles Creed

I believe in God, the Father Almighty, Creator of Heaven and earth;
and in Jesus Christ, His only Son Our Lord,
Who was conceived by the Holy Spirit, born of the Virgin Mary, suffered under Pontius Pilate, was crucified, died, and was buried.
He descended into Hell; the third day He rose again from the dead;
He ascended into Heaven, and sitteth at the right hand of God, the Father almighty; from thence He shall come to judge the living and the dead.
I believe in the Holy Spirit, the holy Catholic Church, the communion of saints, the forgiveness of sins, the resurrection of the body and life everlasting.

Amen.

6. Nicene Creed

I believe in one God,
the Father, the Almighty,
Maker of heaven and earth,
of all things visible and invisible.
I believe in one Lord Jesus Christ,

the only-begotten Son of God,
born of the Father before all ages,
God from God, Light from Light,
true God from true God,
begotten, not made,
consubstantial with the Father.
Through him all things were made.
For us and for our salvation
he came down from heaven:by the power of the Holy Spirit
was incarnate of the Virgin Mary,
and became man.
For our sake he was crucified under Pontius Pilate;
he suffered death and was buried,
and rose again on the third day
in accordance with the Scriptures.
He ascended into heaven
and is seated at the right hand of the Father.
He will come again in glory to judge the living and the dead,
and his kingdom will have no end.
I believe in the Holy Spirit, the Lord, the giver of life,
who proceeds from the Father and the Son.
With the Father and the Son he is adored and glorified.
He has spoken through the Prophets.
I believe in one, holy, catholic and apostolic Church.
I confess one baptism for the forgiveness of sins,
and I look forward to the resurrection of the dead,
and the life of the world to come.
Amen.

7. PENITENTIAL ACT

I confess to almighty God, and to you, my brothers and sisters, that I have greatly sinned through my thoughts and in my words, in what I have done, and in what I have failed to do; through my fault, through my fault, through my most grievous fault; therefore I ask blessed Mary ever-Virgin, all the Angels and Saints, and you, my brothers and sister, to pray for me to the Lord our God.

8. THE GLORIA

Glory to God in the highest, and on earth peace to men of good will. We praise You. we bless You. we adore you. we glorify You. we give You thanks for Your great glory. Lord God, heavenly King, O God, almighty Father. Lord Jesus Christ, the Only Begotten Son. Lord God, Lamb of God, Son of the Father: you Who take away the sins of the world, have mercy on us. You Who take away the sins of the world, receive our prayer. You are seated at the right hand of the Father, have mercy on us. For you alone are the Holy One. You alone are the Lord. You alone are the Most High Jesus Christ. with the Holy Spirit in the glory of God the Father. Amen.

9. An Act of Spiritual Communion

My Jesus, I believe that You are present in the Most Holy Sacrament. I love You above all things, and I desire to receive You into my soul. Since I cannot at this moment receive You sacramentally, come at least spiritually into my heart. I embrace You as if You were already there and unite myself wholly to You. Never permit me to be separated from You. Amen

10. The Angelus

V. The Angel of the Lord declared unto Mary,

R. And she conceived of the Holy Spirit.

Hail Mary, etc...

V. Behold the handmaid of the Lord.

R. Be it done unto me according to Your Word.

Hail Mary, etc...

V. And the Word was made flesh,

R. And dwelt among us.

Hail Mary, etc...
V. Pray for us, O holy Mother of God.
R. That we may be made worthy of the promises of Christ.
Let us pray:
Pour forth, we beseech You, O Lord,
Your Grace into our hearts;
that as we have known the incarnation of Christ,
your Son by the message of an angel,
so by His passion and cross
we may be brought to the glory of His Resurrection.
Through the same Christ, our Lord.
Amen

11. Fatima Prayer

O My Jesus, forgive us our sins, save us from the fires of Hell and lead all souls to Heaven, especially those who are in most need of Thy mercy.

12. The Guardian Angel

Angel of God,
my guardian dear,
To whom God's love
commits me here,
Ever this day,
be at my side,
To light and guard,
Rule and guide.
Amen.

13. Hail Holy Queen

Hail, Holy Queen, Mother of Mercy,
our life, our sweetness and our hope.
To you do we cry,
poor banished children of Eve.
To you do we send up our sighs,
mourning and weeping in this valley of tears

Turn then, most gracious advocate,
your eyes of mercy toward us,
and after this exile
show unto us the blessed fruit of thy womb,
Jesus.
O clement, O loving,
O sweet Virgin Mary.

14. Grace before meal

Bless us, O Lord! and these Thy gifts, which we are about to receive from Thy bounty, through Christ our Lord. Amen.

15. Grace after meal

We give Thee thanks for all Thy benefits, O Almighty God, who livest and reignest world without end. Amen. May the souls of the faithful departed, through the mercy of God, rest in peace. Amen.

16. Regina coeli

Queen of Heaven, rejoice, alleluia!
Because the Son you were chosen to bear, alleluia!
Has risen, as he said, alleluia!
Pray for us to God, alleluia!
Rejoice and be glad, O virgin Mary, alleluia!
Because the Lord is truly risen, alleluia!

O God, who by the Resurrection of your Son, our Lord Jesus Christ, granted joy to the whole world, grant, we beseech you, that through the intercession of the Virgin Mary, his Mother, we may enjoy the happiness of eternal life, through the same Christ Our Lord. Amen.

17. The Memorare

Remember, O most gracious Virgin Mary,
that never was it known
that anyone who fled to thy protection,
implored thy help,

or sought thy intercession,
was left unaided.
Inspired by this confidence
I fly unto thee,
O Virgin of virgins, my Mother.
To thee do I come,
before thee I stand,
sinful and sorrowful.
O Mother of the Word Incarnate,
despise not my petitions,
but in thy mercy hear and answer me.
Amen.

THE ACTS OF PRAYER.

18. ACT OF FAITH

O MY GOD, I firmly believe that Thou art one God in Three Divine Persons, Father, Son and Holy Ghost. I believe that Thy Divine Son became Man, and died for our sins, and that He will come to judge the living and the dead. I believe these and all the truths which the Holy Catholic Church teaches, because Thou hast revealed them, Who canst neither deceive nor be deceived.

19. ACT OF HOPE

O MY GOD, relying on Thy almighty power and infinite mercy and promises, I
hope to obtain pardon of my sins, the help of Thy grace, and Life Everlasting, through the merits of Jesus Christ, my Lord and Redeemer.

20. ACT OF CHARITY

O MY GOD, I love Thee above all things, with my whole heart and soul, because Thou art all-good and worthy of all love. I love my neighbor as myself for the love of Thee. I forgive all who have injured me, and ask pardon of all whom I have injured.

21. ACT OF CONTRITION

O MY GOD, I am heartily sorry for having offended Thee, and I detest all my sins because I dread the loss of Heaven and the pains of Hell; but most of all because they offend Thee, my God, Who art all-good and deserving of all my love. I firmly resolve, with the help of Thy grace, to confess my sins, to do penance, and to amend my life. Amen.

OR

O MY GOD, I am sorry for all my sins because they displease you, who are all good and deserving, of all my love, with your help I will sin no more.

22. Night Prayer

Jesus Christ my God, I adore You and I thank You for all the graces You have given me this day. I offer You my sleep and all the moments of this night, and I implore You to keep me safe from sin. To this end I place myself in Your sacred side and under the mantle of Our Lady, my Mother. Let Your holy angels surround me and keep me in peace; and let Your blessing be upon me.
Amen.

23. Prayer before confession

Receive my confession, O most loving and gracious Lord Jesus Christ, only hope for the salvation of my soul. Grant to me true contrition of soul, so that day and night I may by penance make satisfaction for my many sins. Savior of the world, O good Jesus, Who gave Yourself to the death of the Cross to save sinners, look upon me, most wretched of all sinners; have pity on me, and give me the light to know my sins, true sorrow for them, and a firm purpose of never committing them again.

O gracious Virgin Mary, Immaculate Mother of Jesus, I implore you to obtain for me by your powerful intercession

these graces from your Divine Son.
St. Joseph, pray for me.

24. Prayer after confession

My dearest Jesus, I have told all my sins to the best of my ability. I have sincerely tried to make a good confession and I know that you have forgiven me. Thank you dear Jesus! Your divine heart is full of love and mercy for poor sinners. I love You dear Jesus; you are so good to me. My loving Saviour, I shall try to keep from sin and to love You more each day. Dearest Mother Mary, pray for me and help me to keep all my promises. Protect me and do not let me fall back into sin. Dear God, help me to lead a good life. Without Your grace I can do nothing.
Amen!

25. The Three O'clock Prayer

You expired Jesus, But the source of life gushed forth for souls, and the ocean of mercy opened up for the whole world, O Fount of Life, unfathomable Divine Mercy, envelop the whole world and empty Yourself out upon us. O Blood and Water which gushed forth from the Heart of Jesus as a fount of mercy for us, I trust in you! Holy God, Holy Mighty One, Holy Immortal One, Have Mercy on us and on the whole world. (Say 3 times) Amen.

26. Evening Prayer

Watch, O Lord, with those who wake,
or watch, or weep tonight,
and give Your Angels and Saints charge over those who sleep.
Tend Your sick ones, O Lord Christ.
Rest Your weary ones,
Bless Your dying ones,
Soothe Your suffering ones,
pity Your afflicted ones,

Shield Your joyous ones,
And all for Your love's sake.
Amen.

5
Prayer for Special Intentions

---

1. Prayer to the Holy Spirit

Breathe into me, Holy Spirit, that my thoughts may all be holy. Move in me, Holy Spirit, that my work, too, may be holy. Attract my heart, Holy Spirit, that I may love only what is holy. Strengthen me, Holy Spirit, that I may defend all that is holy. Protect me, Holy Spirit, that I may always be holy.

2. Prayer for peace

Lord Jesus Christ,
You are the true King of peace.
In You alone is found freedom.
Please free our world from conflict.
Bring unity to troubled nations.
Let Your glorious peace reign in every heart.
Dispel all darkness and evil.
Protect the dignity of every human life.
Replace hatred with Your love.
Give wisdom to world leaders.
Free them from selfish ambition.

Eliminate all violence and war.
    Glorious Virgin Mary,
Saint Michael the Archangel,
Every angel and saint:
Please pray for peace.
Pray for unity amongst nations.
Pray for unity amongst all people.
Pray for the most vulnerable.
Pray for those suffering.
Pray for the fearful.
Pray for those most in need.
Pray for us all.
    Jesus, Son of the Living God, have mercy on us.
Jesus, hear our prayers.
Jesus, I trust in You!
    Amen.

3. Prayer for safe journey

Lord, be our guide and our protector
on the journey we are about to take.
Watch over us.
Protect us from accidents.
Keep us free from harm to body and soul.
Lord, support us with Your grace when we are tired.
Help us be patient in any trouble which may come our way.
Keep us always mindful of Your presence and love.
Amen.

4. Prayer before exams

Dear Lord, as I take this exam, I thank you that my value
Is not based on my performance, but on your great love for
me.
Come into my heart so that we can walk through this time
together.
Help me, not only with this test, but the many tests of life

that are sure to come my way.

As I take this exam, bring back to my mind everything I studied and be gracious with what I have overlooked. Help me to remain focused and calm, confident in the facts and in my ability, and firm in the knowledge that no matter what happens today you are there with me.

5. Prayer during exam

Almighty God, please help me in my exams. Help me to face them with courage and peace. Help me to understand the questions that are asked, To remember what I have studied and to express my answers clearly. Guide and direct me in all my decisions and help me especially to discover my true vocation to love and serve you in my life. Lask this through

Christ our Lord. Amen

6. Prayer to studying

Almighty and Everlasting God, I have worked diligently for my upcoming exams. I pray that my hard work pays off in the form of good grades and success. Please guide me towards this success.

Continue to nurture my mind so I can work hard and do well. As I trek towards success please keep my eyes focused on what really matters, Your love. Keep me humble and faithful. Amen.

7. Prayer for priests

Gracious and loving God, we thank you for the gift of our priests.

Through them, we experience your presence in the sacraments.

Help our priests to be strong in their vocation.
Set their souls on fire with love for your people.

Grant them the wisdom, understanding, and strength they need to follow in the footsteps of Jesus.

Inspire them with the vision of your Kingdom.

Give them the words they need to spread the Gospel. Allow them to experience joy in their ministry.

Help them to become instruments of your divine grace.

We ask this through Jesus Christ, who lives and reigns as our Eternal Priest.

Amen.

8. Teenager's Prayer

Glorious One, You have called me to be strong and courageous. I pray that I will not be afraid or terrified because of them, for Lord, You go with me; You will never leave me nor forsake me. Thank You for being my rock and my strength. Thank You for going before me so that I may have the victory at all times. I pray that I walk in Your authority and power, I proclaim strength and fearlessness over my life, Amen.

9. Prayer of Parents

God of life and love, you have given me this child to care for this little while.

My heart is welled with joy and thanksgiving, anticipation and anxiety, amidst a longing to be together as we have been till now.

These years of growing up have moved so quickly, so many things left undone, so much left unsaid, so much I still hope to give to my child who is taking this new step in the journey of life.

Help us as we reshape our lives to reflect this new reality of college. Show us new ways to be present to each other in love and in trust. Give me patience and help me to remember that my child is establishing new routines in freedom, routines different from my routines.

Calm my fears. Strengthen and protect my child in the midst of the challenges and temptations which surround all students. Grant greater courage that I myself may have had in standing for your truth against compromises of faith.

Provide good friends and worthy confidants for my child during these college years. Help me to give support and confidence, to discern how I am needed now, and to pass on, in my love, a measure of the strength and courage you have given me in the gift of parenting. Amen.

10. The Miracle Prayer

Lord Jesus, I come before you, just as I am, I am sorry for my sins, I repent of my sins, please forgive me. In your Name, I forgive all others for what they have done against me. I renounce Satan, the evil spirits and all their works. I give you my entire self, Lord Jesus, now and forever. I invite you into my life, Jesus. I accept you as my Lord, God and Savior. Heal me, change me, strengthen me in body, soul, and spirit.

Come Lord Jesus, cover me with your Precious Blood, and fill me with your Holy Spirit. I love you Lord Jesus. I praise you Jesus. I thank you Jesus. I shall follow you every day of my life. Amen.

Mary, My Mother, Queen of Peace, St. Peregrine, the cancer saint, all the Angels and Saints, please help me. Amen.

[Say this prayer faithfully, no matter how you feel. When you come to the point where you sincerely mean each word with all your heart, Jesus will change your whole life in a very special way. You will see.]

11. In the time of illness

Lord Jesus, you came into the world to heal our infirmities and to endure our sufferings. You went about healing all and bringing comfort to those in pain and need. We come before you now in this time of illness asking that you may be the source of our strength in body, courage in spirit and patience in pain. May we join ourselves more closely to you on the cross and in your suffering that through them we may draw our patience and hope. Assist us and restore us to health so that united more closely to your family, the Church, we may give praise and honour to your name.

Amen.

12. In Disappointments

Dear Heavenly Father, I come to You pleading for You to restore my soul, revive my heart and lead me along the right path for the future, for so much in life has become a disappointment and I know that I have strayed far from You.

Thank You, Lord, for reminding me that my citizenship is in heaven and that the things of this world will only cause me disappointments and distress. Help me to hold lightly to the things of this world and it's enticing possessions, but keep my heart focussed on Jesus, knowing that He will never disappoint me or fail me.

Refresh my weary soul I pray, and may I be like a tree that has been planted by the flowing rivers of life. May I sink my roots deeply into You Lord Jesus, knowing that my hope is in You alone. Fill me I pray, with all hope and joy, and may I draw ever closer to You. In Jesus' name I pray,

Amen.

13. In success

Father, Your positive life-giving energy supersedes any negative-depleting energy inherent in this world. Greater is Who is inside of me than what is in this world. Your Spirit dwells inside of me energizing me to become all You envisioned. I know it is great because what You have envisioned for me is for a bright future paved with one success after another. Amen.

14. For wisdom, courage and Justice.

O God, help me to have in my life the virtuesWhich all persons value and admire.

Give me wisdom always to know, what I ought to to do; What I ought to say; Where I ought to go;

Give me courage, To do the right thing when it is difficult; If need be, to be laughed at for my faith; Never to be ashamed to show my loyalty to you.

Give me justice, Always to be fair in thought, word and action; Always to think of the rights of others
As much as of my own; Never to be content when anyone is being
Unjustly treated;

Give me self-control, Always to have my impulses, passions And emotions under perfect control; Never to be swept into doing things For which I would be sorry; Never to do anything which would hurt others,
Grieve those who love me, Or bring shame to myself.

Hear this my prayer for your love's sake, Amen.

15. On a birthday

Lord, I thank you for giving me the unique opportunity to be able to wish myself a happy birthday in good health and happiness. I pray that You will continue to grant me blessings of love and joy all my life. roach this birthday in the assurance that this is the year in which You will answer my prayers and bless me with a magnificent breakthrough! On this special day, I humbly come before You asking for special blessings. May ill-fortune never come in contact with me. May Your protection and guidance always be with me. I pray that God makes this birthday of mine the most memorable one for myself, my family and my friends. I pray God grants me countless years of excitement, beauty on all sides, and above all, all my heart's desires. Amen.

16. For Basic Things

Lord Jesus, I am grateful for this day that you have made for I am assured you shall fulfill my every need according to your riches in glory. I shall not want for any good or beneficiary necessity. I know the plans you have for me and I praise and worship You that my destiny is established and my dreams shall succeed and You shall grant me the desires of my heart. I awake this morning with Your favor upon my life. Finances are provided ~ Opportunities will find me ~ Doors will be opened ~ Promotions will be granted ~ Advancements will be made ~ Petitions will be granted. I have hope and I'm filled with expectancy each and every day.

In Jesus' Name, Amen!

17. For Friends

Almighty Father, I give thanks today for the friendships in my life. Lord, this life isn't meant to be lived alone, so I am grateful for the people who walk alongside me, supporting me, loving me, and encouraging me. For we cannot do it all alone but are better together. Help me to be more aware and gracious to my friends, appreciating them and accepting their help. Help me to be a better friend, too, supporting, loving, and encouraging others. Lord, lead me to find and cultivate deeper friendships and be a good friend in all that I do. Shower your blessings upon those I call friends, that you may ever be in our midst. Bind us together, Lord, for a cord of three strands is not quickly broken. Amen.

18. A Son's or A Daughter's Prayer

Loving God, you watch over each and every one of your children. Hear my prayer for my father/mother. Be his/her constant companion. Protect him/her no matter where he/she goes, and bring him/her safely and quickly home to those who love him/her. We ask this through Christ our

Lord.

19. For true Friendship

Heavenly, Omnipotent Father, there are times in my life when I need true and genuine friends, a comforting arm, a listening ear, a shoulder to cry on, or even just sensible good advice.

But there are no true friends to turn to. No one who I can relate to or who truly understands exactly how I feel. It leaves me feeling broken, empty, and lost.

Fill me, Lord with Your divine holy presence. Allow me to feel Your tender, warm embrace wrapped around me, as I sit here and cry out to You. Amen

20. For Responsibility

Lord, I pray today for a sense of responsibility. I pray for every father who endows a child with his DNA to take responsibility for that child. Lord, I pray for the fathers of the world; that they might acknowledge the children who carry their seed, but they might also responsible financially and emotionally in the life of their children. Lord, I pray for every mother who has served as a vessel in the passage way of life to live up to her responsibility to raise her children, love her children, and financially support her children, and emotionally interact with her children. Lord, help me with my own sense of responsibility. Teach me to be on time. Teach me to follow through on the commitments I make. Help me not to commit to more than I can deliver. Encourage me not to feel sorry for myself, regardless of how many times I have been let down by others. Fill me with a fire that cannot be quenched. Fill me with a desire to be the best I can be. Fill me with a sense that I can change the world, make a difference in this world, and when I prepare to make my transition from life to life immortal, lay me gently to sleep. Take away the life I have come to know, the breath I have come to depend upon and transport my soul to that world which has no end. Through Jesus Christ our Lord and Savior I pray. Amen.

21. Be with me, Lord

May all I do today begin with you, O Lord. Plant dreams and hopes within my soul, revive my tired spirit: be with me today. May all I do today continue with your help, O Lord. Be at my side and walk with me:

Be my support today. May all I do today reach far and wide, O Lord. My thoughts, my work, my life: make them blessings for your kingdom; let them go beyond today, O God Today is new unlike any other day,

for God makes each day different. Today God's everyday grace falls on my soul like abundant seed,

though I may hardly see it. Today is one of those days Jesus promised to be with me, a companion on my journey, And my life today, if I trust him, has consequences unseen. My life has a purpose. "I have a mission... "I am a link in a chain, a bond of connection between persons. God has not created me for naught... Therefore I will trust him. Whatever, wherever I am, I can never be thrown away. God does nothing in vain. "He knows what he is about." Amen.

22. For Good Habits

O God, help me never to allow
Any habit to get such a grip of me
That I cannot break.

Specially keep me from all habits
Which would injure my body or my mind.

Help me always to do my best with your help
To keep my body fit and healthy,
And my mind clean and pure.

Help me at present to discipline and
Train myself, to learn and to study,

So that some day I may be able to do
Something worthwhile for the world and for You.
This prayer I make for your love's sake, Amen.

23. To spend the day well

My dear and sweet Mother Mary, Co-redemptrix of the human race, keep me in Your holy protection. Guard my mind, my heart and my senses, that I be not stained by sin. Sanctify my thoughts, desires, words, and actions, that I may please You and Your Jesus, my God, and gain paradise with You. Jesus and Mary, give me Your most holy blessing. In the name of the Father, and of the Son, and of the Holy Spirit, One God, forever and ever. Amen

24. A thanksgiving Prayer

Let us remember that we are in the holy presence of God. Loving Creator,
We asked for strength, and you gave us difficulties to make us strong.
We asked for wisdom, and you gave us problems to solve.
We asked for prosperity, and you gave us purpose and brains to use.
We asked for courage, and you gave us fears to overcome.
We asked for patience, and you gave us situations where we were forced to wait.
We asked for love, and you gave us troubled people to help.
We asked for justice, and you called us to be just and to lead with integrity.
Lord, we have received nothing that we asked for or wanted.
And yet, we received everything that we needed.
For this, we give thanks.

25. A Student's Prayer

Lord of Light and Wisdom, thank You for giving me a mind that can know and a heart that can love. Help me to keep learning every day, no matter what the subject is, for all knowledge leads to You.

Encourage me when the studies are hard and when I am tempted to give up. Enlighten me when my brain. is slow, and let me grasp the truth held out to me.

Amen.

26. Daily Prayer

Dear Lord,

I don't know who or what will cross my path today. But I do know that You are my Rock and my Fortress. You are my Shield and my Strong Tower. Help me to anchor myself to You today. Teach me how to stand strong in You and choose only Your way today. Help me walk by Your truth and not my feelings. Help me to embrace anything that comes my way as an opportunity to see You at work and as an opportunity to point others to You. Thank You that You love me and nothing can ever take that away from me! Even if I fail today and fall short, You whisper Your unconditional love deep into my soul and remind me that Your mercies are new every morning. That truly amazes me, Lord. Thank You for meeting with me today. Would You wake me again tomorrow with the same sweet whisper of Your love? I can't wait to meet with You again.

In Jesus' name, Amen.

27. For serenity and courage

God, grant me the serenity
to accept the things I cannot change,
the courage to change the things I can,
and the wisdom to know the difference.
Living one day at a time,
enjoying one moment at a time;
accepting hardship as a pathway to peace;
taking, as Jesus did,
this sinful world as it is,

not as I would have it;
trusting that You will make all things right
if I surrender to Your will;
so that I may be reasonably happy in this life
and supremely happy with You forever in the next.
Amen.

28. For Duties

Help me do my duty to God and put my faith and my trust in him.

To Believe in him and know that he is with me each day.

To put my trust in the Lord and to call upon him for help.

To Honour and Love him with all my Heart and Soul.

To increase my faith with all my strength so that i may worship him without question.

In Spirit and Truth all the days of my life.

Amen

29. Thank you God

Thank you, Lord, for the blessings you have bestowed on my life. You have provided me with more than I could ever have imagined. You have surrounded me with people who always look out for me. You have given me family and friends who bless me every day with kind words and actions. They lift me up in ways that keep my eyes focused on you and make my spirit soar.

Also, thank you, Lord, for keeping me safe. You protect me from those things that seem to haunt others. You help me make better choices and provide me with advisors to help me with life's difficult decisions. You speak to me in so many ways so that I always know you are here. Amen.

30. A teacher's Prayer

Heavenly Father,

Enable me to teach WISDOM,

For I help to shape the mind.

Equip me to teach with TRUTH,
For I help to shape the conscience.
Encourage me to teach with VISION,
For I help to shape the future.
Empower me to teach with LOVE,
For I help to shape the world.
AMEN.

31. Prayer at the beginning of an academic Year

Gracious God, we come to you at the beginning of this academic year with our many feelings, expectations, fears and hopes. Help us to remember, however, we have the comforting assurance from you: "I will always be with you." Loving God, for all of us this is a time of transition. It is transition from the work and leisure of summer back to the classroom. It is transition from time spent with family and friends. Give us patience with ourselves as we transition as well as patience with one another. Amen.

32. Prayer at the end of a term

We thank you Lord, for this term. For our challenges, our successes, and the mistakes from which we have learnt. Be with us as we spend our time with family and friends.

Give us strength and courage to do what is right: to be witnesses of our faith. Help us to be a practical Christian these holidays, to appreciate what others do for us, to give time and effort to help others. To be peacemakers in our family.

Keep us safe in our activities; give us good rest and good fun. Bring us back refreshed and ready for a new term. We thank you for our classmates, teachers, parents and a community that cares for us.

May we always be conscious of you in our lives.

We ask for your richest blessings over Mrs Earl during her sabbatical next term. Surround her with your loving care, keep her safe and return her to us, renewed and refreshed. Amen.

33. For understanding

Lord, teach me how to pray with understanding. Teach me I pray, how to pray into Your will, to pray in spirit and truth, to pray as You would have me pray.

Lord, I ask that as I come across various difficulties that people are facing that I hear with Your ears, see with Your eyes and understand with Your heart so that I may speak and pray into the situation as You would have me pray. In Jesus' name I pray,

Amen.

34. Facing life

Lord, Help me to trust in you with all my heart and not lean on my own understanding but in all my ways submit to you. Make my paths straight and guide me down the right path. I know in this life there will be times of suffering and hardship but help me take heart because I know you have overcome the world.

Give me the courage to face the challenges that come. Help me to persevere and not give up. Give me the strength to face these storms. Pour out your peace over me and keep me in your perfect peace.

I want to always look to you when trials come. Instead of blaming you or looking elsewhere for the answers I want to look to you and trust completely in you. This is hard to do but I ask you to help me surrender everything to you...my emotions, my thoughts, my actions, control.

Thank you, Lord Jesus, for your help through this extremely difficult time. I know you've got this, and you've got me! I praise you and I put all of my faith and trust in you. Thank you, God, for hearing and answering my prayer.

In Jesus Name, Amen.

35. Guide me

O Lord, my God, help me to trust you with my decisions and my future. Let me lean on you with all my heart instead of relying on my own imperfect understanding. Give me clear guidance in my life, Lord. As I submit myself to you, I know that you will direct my paths and I can have confidence that your direction is always the best way to go. Hear my prayer, Father. Through Jesus Christ, our Lord, Amen.

36. For change

Mighty Everlasting Father, everything is changing around me, Oh God: my life, my circumstances and even the world. But, Oh Lord, my God, help me to not fear this change. Rather, may I embrace it as I embrace You daily. Give me strength to rise above every situation and overcome the darkness. Amen

37. For our Country

Almighty God, bless our nation and make it true to the ideas of freedom and justice and brotherhood for all who make it great. Guard us from war, from fire and wind, from compromise, fear, confusion. Be close to our president and our statesmen; give them vision and courage, as they ponder decisions affecting peace and the future of the world. Make me more deeply aware of my heritage; realizing not only my rights but also my duties and responsibilities as a citizen. Make this great land and all its people know clearly Your will, that they may fulfill the destiny ordained for us in the salvation of the nations,
and the restoring of all things in Christ.
Amen

38. For tact

Dear God, please help me to guard my tongue and learn to say the right thing at the right time, for the right reason, in the right way, with the right motive. Help me, too, to know when to seal my lips and keep my mouth shut. Thank you for hearing and answering my prayer. Gratefully, in Jesus' name, Amen.

39. For humility

Lord, We pray for the heart position of humility. Humility in such a way that we do not cheapen our own worth or value within, but that we take the alignment that we are here for a greater purpose than just our own gain. We pray that You will highlight to us what it truly means to live a humble life, and that our own worth will be revealed by Your Light. It is only then that we may truly live in freedom and right standing, for we will hold our own value correctly. Lord, we welcome You to mold and secure our hearts in true humility by Your lead.
In Jesus name, Amen

40. For those in responsible jobs

Lord I pray for me and my job. Please help me have job security and peace on my mind. I put my faith in your hand. I trust and believe in you. You will guide me in the path you have store for me. Thank you for everything you done and will do for me. Amen

41. For honesty

Jesus, Prince of all Heavenly truths, Your Words are carved for eternity! You have commanded the virtue of honesty, It is the power against all deceptions. Direct Your Spirit of honesty upon me, That by soul may always remain stainless. Guide my daily thoughts, words and actions, To join those living by the Spirit of truth. For honesty yields harmony and loyalty, Enriching all human relationships. By the power of Your Spirit that flourishes, Honesty will prevail in this world! Amen.

42. For unity

I rest in you, Spirit of Life.

I place in you my feet, my legs, my torso, my arms, my shoulders, my head and allow you to support all that I am.

I rest in you, Spirit of Life, and give to you my worries, my fears, my doubts, my hopes, my joys, my pains, my anger, my love, my hate, and allow you to take in all that I am.

And as I give all that I am, I find the place of truth, stillness, still, eternal where you and I are one.

I breathe in, deep, deeply, down, up, all that we are, as I stand on my toe at the edge of the universe, in oneness.

And all that we are expands, until forever. Amen.

43. For the Family

Lord God, I give you all the members of our family. You know them all so well and love them all. I ask that you would cover us with a rainbow of hope.

Hope that draws us together to work out our differences.

Hope that helps us to celebrate together and care for one another.

Hope that rides like a banner in our lives and watches over us wherever we go.

Hope that overcomes adversity and gathers strength to overcome.

Hope that guides us and gives us vision for our future alone and together.

Hope filled with love.

Hope that fuels faith.

Hope that breathes peace.

May our family live in you

Underneath your promises. Amen.

44. For Forgiveness

Lord Jesus, for too long I've kept you out of my life. I know that I am a sinner and that I cannot save myself. No longer will I close the door when I hear you knocking. By faith I gratefully receive your gift of salvation. I am ready to trust you as my Lord and Savior. Thank you, Lord Jesus, for coming to earth. I believe you are the Son of God who died on the cross for my sins and rose from the dead on the third day. Thank you for bearing my sins and giving me the gift of eternal life. I believe your words are true. Come into my heart, Lord Jesus, and be my Savior. Amen.

45. For Enlightenment

O Holy Ghost, divine Spirit of light and love, I consecrate to Thee my understanding, my heart and my will, my whole being for time and for eternity. May my understanding be always obedient to Thy heavenly inspirations and the teachings of the holy Catholic Church, of which Thou art the infallible Guide; may my heart be ever inflamed with love of God and of my neighbor; may my will be ever conformed to the divine will, and may my whole life be a faithful following of the life and virtues of Our Lord and Savior Jesus Christ, to whom with the Father and Thee be honor and glory for ever. Amen.

46. For the dead

God our Father, Your power brings us to birth, Your providence guides our lives, and by Your command we return to dust. Lord, those who die still live in Your presence, their lives change but do not end. I pray in hope for my family, relatives and friends, and for all the dead known to You alone. In company with Christ,
Who died and now lives, may they rejoice in Your kingdom, where all our tears are wiped away. Unite us together again in one family, to sing Your praise forever and ever.
Amen.

47. For a newly married couple

Father, you are Love and Life.

Through your Son, Jesus Christ, born of woman, and through the Holy Spirit, fountain of divine charity, grant that every family on earth may become for each successive generation a true shrine of life and love.

Grant that your grace may guide the thoughts and actions of husbands and wives for the good of their families and of all the families in the world.

Grant that the young may find in the family solid support for their human dignity and for their growth in truth and love.

Grant that love, strengthened by the grace of the sacrament of marriage, may prove mightier than all the weakness and trials through which our families sometimes pass.

Through the intercession of the Holy Family of Nazareth, grant that the Church may fruitfully carry out her worldwide mission in the family and through the family.

Through Christ our Lord, who is the Way, the Truth and the Life for ever and ever.

Amen

48. For courage to face our fears.

Lord, so often I fail to acknowledge Your divine presence in my life. So often I fail to see you coming to me. Help me to know that You are always there. Free me from the many fears of life, dear Lord, and give me courage to welcome You fully into my life. Jesus, I trust in You. Amen

49. For a newly baptised child

Dear God, send your Holy Spirit daily to lead, guide and counsel my child. Always assist him or her to grow in wisdom and stature, in grace and knowledge, in kindness, compassion, and love. May this child serve you faithfully, with his whole heart devoted to you all the days of his life.

May he discover the joy of your presence through a daily relationship with your Son, Jesus Christ.

50. For victory in a game

Dear Father! I praise You and honour You as my Lord! You are in control of all things! Even now Lord You know how important this sports event is for me.Lord! The Scripture says that we are more than conquerors through You. You are the only all powerful and wise God. I trust You to grant me victory in this field O Lord it is nothing for You to help a weak person. I do not rely on my strength or ability Lord! I humble myself and I choose to place all my confidence in You and none in my flesh.Lord! Grant me robust health and keep me physically fit to achieve success in my efforts. Let Your name alone be glorified through my victory Lord! Please let me prove to the world that I am the child of the Almighty.I have the confidence that I can do everything through You. Strengthen me O Lord and let me shine for Your glory. Protect me from all harm and danger. I pray all this in the most precious name of Jesus my Saviour, Lord and friend.Amen.

51. To make your plan a success

Lord, Jesus Christ, thank you that every good and perfect gift comes from you, the King of kings and Lord of lords. You have promised that, if I commit whatever I do to you, then you will cause my plans to succeed. My success will come from aligning my plans with your will. Let me hear your voice clearly as you give me wisdom and guidance. Remind me that success is not found in the world but is found in you. Now may you, the Lord of all, give me success at all times and in every way. In your mighty name, Amen.

6
Prayer for Saints

1. Prayer to St Joseph

Oh St. Joseph whose protection is so great, so strong, so prompt before the throne of God, I place in you all my interests and desires. Oh St. Joseph do assist me by your powerful intercession and obtain for me from your divine son all spiritual blessings through Jesus Christ, our Lord; so that having engaged here below your heavenly power I may offer my thanksgiving and homage to the most loving of fathers. Oh St. Joseph, I never weary contemplating you and Jesus asleep in your arms. I dare not approach while he reposes near your heart. Press him in my name and kiss his fine head for me, and ask him to return the kiss when I draw my dying breath. St. Joseph, patron of departing souls, pray for us.

Amen.

2. Prayer to St. Anthony

IF then you ask for miracles,
Death, error, all calamities,
The leprous stain and demons fly,
And health succeeds infirmities.

The sea obeys and fetters break,
And lifeless limbs thou dost restore:
Whilst treasures lost are found again,
When young or old thine aid implore.
　All dangers vanish at thy prayer,
And direst need doth quickly flee,
Let those who know, thy power proclaim
Let Paduans say—These are of thee.
　Repeat: The sea obeys, etc.
　To the Father, Son, may glory be,
And Holy Spirit eternally.
　Repeat: The sea obeys, etc.
　V) Pray for us, St Anthony.
R) That we may be made worthy of the promises of Christ.
　LET US PRAY
　O God, may the votice solemnity (commemoration) of St Anthony, Thy confessor, and Doctor give joy to the Church that it may be ever defended by spiritual aid and deserve to enjoy eternal happiness. Through Christ Our Lord. Amen.

3. St. Teresa of Child Jesus

O Little Therese of the Child Jesus Please pick for me a rose from the heavenly garden and send it to me as a message of love.

O Little Flower of Jesus, ask God to grant the favors I now place with confidence in you hands (mention your special prayer request here)

St. Therese, help me to always believe as you did, in God's great love for me, so that I may imitate your "Little Way" each day. Amen.

4. Canonization of Mother Teresa

Jesus, you made Mother Teresa an inspiring example of firm faith and burning charity,
An extraordinary witness to the way of spiritual childhood,

And a great esteemed teacher of the value and dignity of
every human life.
Grant that she may be venerated and imitated
As one of the Church's canonized saints.
Hear the requests of all those who seek her intercession,
Especially the petition I now implore...
(mention here the favour you wish to pray for).
May we follow her example in heeding Your cry of thirst
from the cross
And joyfully loving You in the distressing disguise of the
poorest of the poor,
Especially those most unloved and unwanted.
We ask this in Your name and through the intercession of
Mary,
Your Mother and the Mother of us all.
Amen.

5. Prayer to St. Michael

St. Michael the Archangel, defend us in battle, be our
protection against the wickedness and snares of the devil.
May God rebuke him we humbly pray; and do thou, O
Prince of the Heavenly host, by the power of God, cast into
hell Satan and all the evil spirits who prowl about the world
seeking the ruin of souls.
Amen.

6. Prayer to St. Dominic

O God, you have enlightened your Church by the
eminent virtues and preaching of St. Dominic, your
confessor.

Mercifully grant that by his prayers we may be protected
against temporal necessities and daily improve in all that is
spiritually good.

Jesus, Mary and Joseph most kind, bless us now and at
the hour of our death.

O Lord, deliver us from a sudden and unprovided death. Amen.

7. Prayer to St. Peter

O Glorious Saint Peter, who, in return for thy strong and generous faith, thy profound and sincere humility,
and thy burning love, was rewarded by Jesus Christ with singular privileges, and, in particular, with the leadership of the other Apostles and the primacy of the whole Church, of which you were made the foundation stone, obtain for us the grace of a lively faith, that shall not fear to profess itself openly, in its entirety and in all of its manifestations, even to the shedding of blood, if occasion should demand it, and to sacrifice of life itself rather than surrender. Obtain for us likewise, a sincere loyalty to our holy mother, the Church; grant that we may ever remain most closely and sincerely united to the Roman Pontiff, who is the heir of thy faith and of thy authority, the one, true, visible Head of the Catholic Church. Grant, moreover, that we may follow, in all humility and meekness, her teaching and her advice, and may be obedient to all her precepts, in order to be able here on earth to enjoy a peace that is sure and undisturbed, and to attain one day in heaven to everlasting happiness. Amen.

8. Prayer to St. John Bosco

O glorious Saint John Bosco, who in order to lead young people to the feet of the divine Master and to mould them in the light of faith and Christian morality didst heroically sacrifice thyself to the very end of thy life and didst set up a proper religious Institute destined to endure and to bring to the farthest boundaries of the earth thy glorious work, obtain also for us from Our Lord a holy love for young people who are exposed to so many seductions in order that we may generously spend ourselves in supporting them against the snares of the devil, in keeping them safe from the dangers of the world, and in guiding them, pure and holy, in the path that leads to God. Amen.

9. Prayer to St. Charles Borromeo

Almighty God, you have generously made known to man the mysteries of your life through Jesus Christ your Son in the Holy Spirit. Enlighten my mind to know these mysteries which your Church treasures and teaches.

Move my heart to love them and my will to live in accord with them. Give me the ability to teach this Faith to others without pride, without ostentation, and without personal gain.

Let me realize that I am simply your instrument for bringing others to the knowledge of the wonderful things you have done for all your creatures. Help me to be faithful to this task that you have entrusted to me. Amen.

10. Prayer to Agatha of Sicily

O Saint Agatha,
you resisted unwelcome advances from unwanted suitors,
and suffered pain and torture for your devotion to our Lord
Jesus Christ;
we celebrate your faith, dignity and martyrdom.

Protect us from sexual and other violations,
guard us against all afflictions,
and inspire us to overcome adversity.

Saint Agatha, virgin and martyr,
mercifully grant that we who venerate your sacrifice
may receive your intercession in times of need. Amen.

11. Prayer to Agnes of Rome

O Little St. Agnes,
so young and yet made so strong
and wise by the power of God,
protect by your prayers
all the young people of every place

whose goodness and purity are threatened by the evils
and impurities of this world.

Give them strength in temptation
and a true repentance when they fail.
Help them to find true Christian friends
to accompany them in following the Lamb of God
and finding safe pastures in His Church
and in her holy sacraments.

May you lead us
to the wedding banquet of heaven
to rejoice with you and all the holy virgin martyrs in Christ
who lives and reigns forever and ever. Amen.

12. Prayer to Albert the Great

We pray to You, O Lord,
who are the supreme Truth,
and all truth is from you.

We beseech You, O Lord,
who are the highest Wisdom,
and all the wise depend on You for their wisdom.
You are the supreme Joy,
and all who are happy owe it to You.
You are the Light of minds,
and all receive their understanding from You.
We love, we love You above all.
We seek You, we follow You,
and we are ready to serve You.
We desire to dwell under Your power
for You are the King of all. Amen.

13. Prayer to Alphonsus Liguori

My Jesus, I believe that You are present in the Blessed
Sacrament. I love You above all things and I desire You
in my soul. Since I cannot now receive You sacramentally,
come at least spiritually into my heart. As though You were

already there, I embrace You and unite myself wholly to You; permit not that I should ever be separated from You. Amen.

14. Prayer to Andrew The Apostle

O Glorious St. Andrew,
you were the first to recognize and follow the Son of God.
With your friend, St. John,
you remained with Jesus,
for your entire life,
and now throughout eternity.

Just as you led your brother, St Peter,
to Christ and many others after him,
draw us also to Him.
Teach us how to lead them,
solely out of love for Jesus
and dedication to His service.
Help us to learn the lesson of the Cross
and carry our daily crosses without complaint,
so that they may carry us to God the Almighty Father.
Amen.

15. Prayer to Archangel Gabriel

Blessed Archangel Gabriel, we beseech thee. Intercede for us at the throne of Divine Mercy in our present necessities, that as you announced to Mary the mystery of the Incarnation, so through thy prayers and patronage in heaven we may obtain the same benefits, and sing the praise of God forever in the land of the living. Amen.

16. Prayer to Archangel Raphael

Blessed Saint Raphael, Archangel, we beseech you to help us in all our needs and trials of this life, as you, through the power of God, did restore sight and gave guidance to young Tobit. We humbly seek your aid and intercession, that our souls may be healed, our bodies protected from all ills, and that through divine grace we may become fit to dwell in the eternal Glory of God in heaven. Amen.

17. Prayer to Catherine of Siena

Holy Spirit, come into my heart;
draw it to Thee by Thy power, O my God,
and grant me charity with filial fear.
Preserve me, O beautiful love, from every evil thought;
warm me, inflame me with Thy dear love, and every pain will seem light to me.
My Father, my sweet Lord, help me in all my actions.
Jesus, love, Jesus, love. Amen.

18. Prayer to Dominic Savio

O Saint Dominic Savio, a model of purity, piety, penance and apostolic zeal for youth; grant that, through your intercession, we may service God in our ordinary duties with fervent devotion, and attain the grace of holy joy on earth, that we may one day love God forever in Heaven. Amen.

19. Prayer to Francis de Sales

Do not look forward in fear to the changes in life;
rather, look to them with full hope that as they arise,
God, whose very own you are, will lead you safely through all things; and when you cannot stand it, God will carry you in His arms. Do not fear what may happen tomorrow; the same understanding Father who cares for you today will take care of you then and every day. He will either shield you from suffering or will give you unfailing strength to bear it. Be at peace, and put aside all anxious thoughts and imaginations. Amen.

20. Prayer to Faustina Kowalska

O Jesus, who filled your handmaid St Faustina with profound veneration for your boundless Mercy, design, if it be Your holy will, to grant me, through her intercession the grace for which I fervently pray:

(Share your request...)

My sins render me unworthy of your mercy, but be mindful of St Faustina's spirit of sacrifice and self-denial, and reward her virtue by granting the petition which, with childlike confidence, I present to You through her intercession.

21. Prayer to Francis of Assisi

Whoever shall observe these things may he be filled in heaven with the blessing of the most-high Father, and may he be filled on earth with the blessing of his beloved son, together with the Holy Spirit, the Consoler, and all the powers of heaven and all the saints.

And I, brother Francis, your worthless servant, as far as I am able, approve this most-holy blessing both internally and externally. Amen.

22. Prayer to Francis Xavier

Eternal God, Creator of all things, remember that You alone created the souls of unbelievers, which You have made according to Your Image and Likeness.

Behold, O Lord, how to Your dishonour many of them are falling into Hell.

Remember, O Lord, Your Son Jesus Christ, Who so generously shed His Blood and suffered for them.

Do not permit that Your Son, Our Lord, remain unknown by unbelievers, but, with the help of Your Saints and the Church, the Bride of Your Son, remember Your mercy, forget their idolatry and infidelity, and make them know Him, Who You have sent, Jesus Christ, Your Son, Our Lord,

Who is our salvation, our life, and our resurrection, through Whom we have been saved and redeemed, and to Whom is due glory forever. Amen.

23. Prayer to Gerard Majella

Almighty and loving Father, I thank you for giving St. Gerard to us as a great role model and powerful friend.

Through his example, he has shown us how to love and trust You.

You shower many blessings on those who call upon his assistance.

For Your greater glory and my welfare, please grant me the favours which I now ask in his name.

(Share your request...)

And you, my powerful patron, intercede for me before the throne of God.

Draw near to His throne and do not leave until you have been heard.

O Good Saint, to you I address my fervent prayers; graciously accept them and let me experience in some way the effects of your powerful intercession. Amen.

24. Prayer to Ignatius of Loyola

Lord, teach me to be generous.

Teach me to serve you as you deserve;

to give and not to count the cost,

to fight and not to heed the wounds,

to toil and not to seek for rest,

to labour and not to ask for reward,

save that of knowing that I do your will. Amen.

25. Prayer to Maria Goretti

O Saint Maria Goretti who, strengthened by God's grace, did not hesitate even at the age of eleven to shed your blood and sacrifice life itself to defend your virginal purity.

Look graciously on the unhappy human race which has strayed far from the path of eternal salvation.

Teach us all, especially the youth, to flee from anything that could offend Jesus and stain our souls with sin.

Obtain for us from our Lord, victory in temptation, comfort in the sorrows of life, and the grace which we now earnestly beg of thee... (Share your request)...

St Maria, pray that we may one day enjoy with you, the eternal glory of Heaven. Amen.

26. Prayer to Vincent de Paul

St. Vincent, patron of all charitable associations and father of those who are in misery, come to our assistance. Obtain from Our Lord, help for the poor, relief for the infirm, consolation for the afflicted, protection for the abandoned, a spirit of generosity for the rich, grace of conversion for sinners, zeal for priests, peace for the Church, tranquillity and order for all nations, and salvation for them all.

May we be united in the life to come, by your intercession, and experience joy, gladness, and everlasting happiness. Amen.

Confession

In modern times the Roman Catholic Church teaches that confession, or reconciliation, is a sacrament, instituted by Christ, in which a confession of all serious sins committed after baptism is necessary.

7
Order of confession

————•♡•————

1. Getting Ready for Confession

1. <u>Examine your conscience.</u> Since you're going to confession and all, you probably want to have an idea of what to say! Sitting back and reflecting on your actions is referred to as "an examination of conscience." So take a moment to call to mind your behavior since your last confession -- from the smallest to the largest of sins. If you wish to pray to the Holy Spirit during this time for guidance, you may. Don't know where to start? Here are a few questions you can ponder:

- Have I disobeyed any of the commandments?
- Have I nourished my faith?
- Has anything else in my life influenced me more than God?
- Have I denied or doubted my faith?
- Have I hurt others, either accidentally or purposefully?
- Have I rejected any part of my faith?
- Have I been forgiving?

- What are the causes of my sins?
- What temptations do I surround myself with?

2. <u>Understand the difference between mortal and venial sin.</u> Most of us commit venial sins on the regular; they're nothing to be ashamed of, though forgiveness should still be sought. These are your everyday sins -- lying to a friend to get out of a party, using God's name in vain, etc. Then there are the mortal sins, which are no laughing matter. Three conditions must be present in order for a sin to be mortal:

- It must involve grave matter.
- You must understand what you're doing at the time you're doing it.
- You must have done it according to your own free will.
- Keep in mind that whatever it is, your priest will keep your secrets. Whatever it is, he will not (and cannot) pass judgment or let your secrets out. Even under threat of death! He can be trusted. You needn't worry about the consequences of telling him. In fact, neglecting to tell him is a sin in itself!
- Unfortunately many people think they could easily commit a mortal sin which makes them intimidated and thus leads to scrupulosity and eventually, OCD. This is a misconception. The good news is most sins are venial because many people don't understand what grave matter means in the criteria of mortal sins. Grave matter means the sin has to be severe. For example, grave matter includes murder, rape, selling illegal drugs or illegal drug abuse, adultery (a fancy term for "cheating" on your wife or husband), incest (To be married or have sexual intercourse with family, cousins, or relatives), theft of very expensive merchandise or stealing a huge

portion of money, extreme hatred to your parents such as wishing them death. Venial sins are minor sins even if they were committed with knowledge and consent. This means you cannot commit a mortal sin if either the sin you committed was not grave even if you chose to do it anyway and with full knowledge, or if it did involve grave matter, but you were neither aware of what you were doing was a grave matter or you were forced to do it. No number of venial sins could ever become a mortal sin. Venial sins include petty theft (stealing something cheap), arguing with siblings, fighting someone for having a different opinion, speeding, etc. now just because you won't go to Hell, venial sins are to be avoided at all costs.

3. <u>Find a confession session.</u> This can either be done by dropping in or making a phone call; many churches have designated times for confessions. Though a priest can usually be found at most times with enough looking, going to a scheduled session is easiest. However, a quick phone call or brief meeting and you can schedule a private session as well.

- If you're nervous to go into the church, don't be! Many churches have publicized when confession is -- either on a sign outside the church or as part of the church bulletin, which can almost always be found at the entrances. Some are even up online!
- Private sessions are a good idea if you have a lot to talk about. A normal confession may last 10 or so minutes. If you think yours will last a lot longer, feel free to ask for a private session.

4. <u>Pray that you may be honest and repentant.</u> It's always a good idea to do a little prayer before confession to ensure that all goes well, nothing escapes your memory, and to ensure that your penitence is meaningful and true. You want to go in with nothing but the best of intentions.

- A large part of a good confession is meaning it, is seeking forgiveness, is putting your heart and soul into it. Even if you sat down with the priest and only muttered out an, "I hurt my friend" between sobs of regret, that'd be so much better than listing out every sin you've committed since your last confession between eye rolls. It's all about being true and faithful. The act of confession is about contrition -- wholly rejecting sin.

2. Talking to the Priest

1. <u>Enter the church and take your seat in a pew.</u> You could go directly into the confessional (provided there's no one else in there or waiting outside), but sometimes it's nice to take a minute in the pew by yourself beforehand. You have this beautiful church probably almost all to yourself. Can you feel its energy resonating through you? Can you feel the majesty of the Lord's kingdom and how you're a part of it?

- Take a moment to kneel and pray with your head down and hands clasped together. Reflect on your faith and how you feel currently. Think about how you've been responding to God's call and how you've been living in the light of his love.

2. <u>Enter the confessional.</u> When the priest is ready for you, of course. You'll probably see him there by his lonesome or someone else walk out just before you. Sit down either across from him or behind the screen -- it's totally up to you whether or not you prefer to remain anonymous. He won't treat you any differently either way.

- Make the sign of the cross upon his prompt, saying, "Bless me, Father, for I have sinned. It has been (blank) since my last confession." This is your standard, traditional phrasing. However, if you just sit down and say hello, that's fine, too. The priest knows what he's doing.
- The Byzantine Rite is a bit different. The priest may sit to your side and put his epitrachelion on your head. He may then also do the Prayer of Absolution. But the idea remains the exact same -- just go wherever he takes you.

3. <u>Follow the priest's lead.</u> Once you sit down and you've made the sign of the cross, just sit back and follow the priest's lead. He'll ask you how long it's been since your last confession (if you don't voluntarily offer that information), how you are feeling, maybe how your faith is going, and then ask you what sins you would like to talk about with him and God. It's just a casual conversation!

- Do not fret. There is absolutely zero pressure on your part. Again, as long as you come there with the intention of leaving with a clean heart, you're more than welcome in the church. There is no wrong way to go about confession!

4. <u>Confess your sins.</u> This part is intimidating, but think about it this way: the priest you're talking to has probably heard just about everything before. Whatever you have to say will not blow his mind. So when he asks, start rattling them off, from the most serious to the least. If he asks any questions, answer them, but do not feel the need to go into detail. A simple, "I did so and so," will suffice.

- Your priest is going to be very understanding. If you don't remember the exact timeframe, that's fine. If you don't remember your motivation, that's fine. All your priest cares about is that you're being as honest as possible and that your heart is in the right place.

5. <u>Listen as the priest offers counsel.</u> He'll talk you through everything, possibly asking about your intentions, but mainly just letting you know that God loves you, sin and all. If he has any ideas to bring you closer to God, he may suggest them at this juncture. He's there to help, after all. He will then ask you to make an Act of Contrition. That goes like this:

- My God, I am sorry for my sins with all my heart. In choosing to do wrong and failing to do good, I have sinned against You whom I should love above all things. I firmly intend, with your help, to do penance, to sin no more, and to avoid whatever leads me to sin. Our Savior Jesus Christ suffered and died for us. In his name, my God, have mercy
- (If you are a Roman Catholic, your act of contrition will go like this:
- Oh my God, I am very sorry for having offended thee. I detest all of my sins because of thy just punishment. But

most of all, because they offend you, my God, who is all good and deserving of all my love. I firmly resolve with the help of thy grace, to sin no more, and to avoid the near occasion of sin. Amen.

6. <u>Take heed as the priest will then offer absolution and recommend penance.</u> Don't worry! It won't be anything huge. You may even walk away just having to say a few meaningful prayers. Take the absolution to heart -- you now have a brand new, clean slate to work with. It'll feel so uplifting!

- Just to clarify, "absolution" means your sins are washed away. "Penance" is your expression of regret and repentance, showing God that you're truly sorry for what you've done and that you wish for nothing more than to be forgiven.

3. Sealing the Deal

1. <u>Leave the confessional feeling a little lighter than before.</u> The priest will give you a "Go in peace to love and serve the Lord," or something very similar. Smile, thank him, walk out, and be excited! Your sins have been forgiven and you have a clean slate to work with. You're that much closer to God. Can you feel it? Now what are you going to do with your fresh start?

- If you forgot a sin you wished to mention, don't fret. God knows of your intentions and it has been forgiven along with the others. However, you may want to mention it next time. Or it could fester and turn into some unnecessary guilt!

2. <u>If you wish, return to your pew.</u> Many often choose to return to their pew and resume prayer, offering a silent thanks to God. And if your penance was a select number of certain prayers, there's no better time than now to channel God. So feel free to return to your seat and bookend your reconciliation with prayer.

- Many reflect on their experiences and how they can avoid the sins in the future. When's the next time you plan on confessing? What can you do in the meantime to find inspiration to live in His image? Harden your resolve now to try to live as He intended.

3. <u>Complete your penance.</u> Whatever the priest suggested you do for penance is best completed as soon as possible. Whether that's in the pew or a conversation you need to have with a loved one, seek to fulfill His desires as soon as possible. You'll feel so relieved when all is said and done!

- Upon completion of your penance, you may want to take a moment to thank God and revel in your absolution. Think about how much God loves you and how wonderful it is to be a part of His glory. Not everyone is so lucky!

4. <u>Pledge to stay aligned with God.</u> It is not expected that you never sin again. God knows that's ridiculous! It's only expected that you seek to avoid the situations that lead you to sin. It's also not wise to view confession as an excuse to sin! No, no, no. Confession is just a part of bringing

humanity a bit closer to God, imperfections and all. All He wants is for you to do your best.

- As you go about the next days and weeks, keep in mind God's part in your life and how you can strive to live as He desires. Seek out the scriptures for inspiration, and surround yourself with those who yearn to live in similar ways. In other words? Go forth to love and serve the Lord. Your Lord.

Rosary

Rosary beads are used to help Catholics count their prayers. Catholics often pray the rosary to make a request to God, some to thank God for blessings received or for requesting a special favour, for example if someone is sick to help them recover.

8
How to Pray The Rosary

1. On the crucifix (cross), make the sign of the cross and then pray the Apostles' Creed.

I believe in God, the Father Almighty, Creator of Heaven and earth; and in Jesus Christ, His only Son, Our Lord, Who was conceived by the Holy Ghost, born of the Virgin Mary, suffered under Pontius Pilate, was crucified; died, and was buried. He descended into Hell; the third day He arose again from the dead; He ascended into Heaven, sitteth at the right hand of God, the Father Almighty; from thence He shall come to judge the living and the dead. I believe in the Holy Spirit, the holy Catholic Church, the communion of saints, the forgiveness of sins, the resurrection of the body, and life everlasting. Amen.

2. On the next large bead, say the Our Father.

Our Father, Who art in heaven, hallowed be Thy name; Thy kingdom come; Thy will be done on earth as it is in heaven. Give us this day our daily bread; and forgive us our trespasses as we forgive those who trespass against us; and lead us not into temptation, but deliver us from evil, Amen.

3. On the following three small beads, pray three Hail Mary's.

Hail Mary, full of grace. The Lord is with thee. Blessed art thou among women, and blessed is the fruit of thy womb, Jesus. Holy Mary, Mother of God, pray for us sinners, now and at the hour of our death. Amen.

4. On the chain, pray The Glory Be.

Glory be to the Father, to the Son, and to the Holy Spirit, as it was, is now, and ever shall be, world without end. Amen.

5. On the large bead, meditate on the first mystery and pray the Our Father.

You pray mysteries for each of the five sections (decades) of the rosary according to the day of the week:

- Mondays and Saturdays: The Joyful Mysteries
- Tuesdays and Fridays: The Sorrowful Mysteries
- Wednesdays and Sundays: The Glorious Mysteries
- Thursdays:

6. Skip the centerpiece medallion, and on the ten beads after that, pray a Hail Mary on each bead; on the chain, pray a Glory Be.

Although a decade is 10, these 12 prayers form a decade of the rosary.

Many Catholics add the Fatima Prayer after the Glory Be and before the next Our Father: O My Jesus, forgive us our sins, save us from the fires of hell and lead all souls to heaven, especially those in most need of Thy mercy. Amen.

7. Repeat Steps 5 and 6 four more times to finish the next four decades.

8. At the end of your Rosary, say the Hail Holy Queen.

Hail, Holy Queen, Mother of mercy, our life, our sweetness, and our hope. To thee do we cry, poor banished children of Eve, to thee do we send up our sighs, mourning and weeping in this valley of tears. Turn then, most gracious advocate, thine eyes of mercy toward us; and after this our exile show unto us the blessed fruit of thy womb Jesus, O clement, O loving, O sweet Virgin Mary.

Pray for us, O holy Mother of God. That we may be made worthy of the promises of Christ.

O God, whose only-begotten Son, by His life, death, and resurrection, has purchased for us the rewards of eternal salvation; grant we beseech Thee, that meditating upon these mysteries of the most holy Rosary of the Blessed Virgin Mary, we may imitate what they contain and obtain what they promise. Through the same Christ our Lord. Amen.

9

Mysteries

Joyful Mysteries

Mondays and Saturdays

1. The Annunciation (Luke 1:26–38);
2. The Visitation (Luke 1:39–56);
3. The Nativity (Luke 2:1–21);
4. The Presentation (Luke 2:22–38);
5. The Finding of the Child Jesus in the Temple (Luke 2:41–52)

Sorrowful Mysteries

Tuesdays and Fridays

1. The Agony of Jesus in the Garden (Matthew 26:36–56);

2. The Scourging at the Pillar (Matthew 27:26);
3. The Crowning with Thorns (Matthew 27:27–31);
4. The Carrying of the Cross (Matthew 27:32);
5. The Crucifixion (Matthew 27:33–56).

·

Glorious Mysteries

Wednesdays and Sundays

1. The Resurrection (John 20:1–29);
2. The Ascension (Luke 24:36–53);
3. The Descent of the Holy Spirit (Acts 2:1–41);
4. The Assumption of Mary, the Mother of God, into heaven;
5. The Coronation of Mary in heaven.

·

Luminous Mysteries

Thursdays

1. The Baptism in the River Jordan (Matthew 3:13–16);
2. The Wedding Feast at Cana (John 2:1–11);
3. The Preaching of the coming of the Kingdom of God (Mark 1:14–15);
4. The Transfiguration (Matthew 17:1–8);
5. The Institution of the Holy Eucharist (Matthew 26).

10
Litany to the Blessed Virgin Mary

Lord, have mercy on us.
Christ, have mercy on us.
Lord, have mercy on us.
Christ, hear us.
Christ, graciously hear us.
God the Father of Heaven,
Have mercy on us.
God the Son, Redeemer of the world,
Have mercy on us.
God the Holy Ghost,
Have mercy on us.
Holy Trinity, one God,
Have mercy on us.
Holy Mary,
pray for us.
Holy Mother of God,
pray for us.
Holy Virgin of virgins,
pray for us.

Mother of Christ,
pray for us.
Mother of divine grace,
pray for us.
Mother most pure,
pray for us.
Mother most chaste,
pray for us.
Mother inviolate,
pray for us.
Mother undefiled,
pray for us.
Mother most amiable,
pray for us.
Mother most admirable,
pray for us.
Mother of good counsel,
pray for us.
Mother of our Creator,
pray for us.
Mother of our Savior,
pray for us.
Virgin most prudent,
pray for us.
Virgin most venerable,
pray for us.
Virgin most renowned,
pray for us.
Virgin most powerful,
pray for us.
Virgin most merciful,
pray for us.
Virgin most faithful,

pray for us.
Mirror of justice,
pray for us.
Seat of wisdom,
pray for us.
Cause of our joy,
pray for us.
Spiritual vessel,
pray for us.
Vessel of honor,
pray for us.
Singular vessel of devotion,
pray for us.
Mystical rose,
pray for us.
Tower of David,
pray for us.
Tower of ivory,
pray for us.
House of gold,
pray for us.
Ark of the Covenant,
pray for us.
Gate of Heaven,
pray for us.
Morning star,
pray for us.
Health of the sick,
pray for us.
Refuge of sinners,
pray for us.
Comforter of the afflicted,
pray for us.

Help of Christians,
pray for us.
Queen of angels,
pray for us.
Queen of patriarchs,
pray for us.
Queen of prophets,
pray for us.
Queen of apostles,
pray for us.
Queen of martyrs,
pray for us.
Queen of confessors,
pray for us.
Queen of virgins,
pray for us.
Queen of all saints,
pray for us.
Queen conceived without Original Sin,
pray for us.
Queen assumed into Heaven,
pray for us.
Queen of the most holy Rosary,
pray for us.
Queen of peace,
pray for us.

Lamb of God, who takes away the sins of the world,
Spare us, O Lord.
Lamb of God, who takes away the sins of the world,
Graciously hear us, O Lord.
Lamb of God, who takes away the sins of the world,
Have mercy on us.

Pray for us, O Holy Mother of God,
That we may be made worthy of the promises of Christ.
Grant, we beseech Thee, O Lord God, that we Thy Servants may enjoy perpetual health of mind and body and by the glorious intercession of the Blessed Mary, ever Virgin, be delivered from present sorrow and enjoy eternal happiness. Through Christ Our Lord.

    Amen.

Stations of the Cross

Stations of the Cross, also called Way of the Cross, a series of 14 pictures or carvings portraying events in the Passion of Christ, from his condemnation by Pontius Pilate to his entombment.

11

Stations of the Cross

Opening Prayer

O MY GOD, I am sorry for all my sins because they displease you, who are all good and deserving, of all my love, with your help I will sin no more.

1. Jesus is condemned to death

Jesus, you stand all alone before Pilate. Nobody speaks up for you. Nobody helps defend you. You devoted your entire life to helping others, listening to the smallest ones, caring for those who were ignored by others. They don't seem to remember that as they prepare to put you to death.

Leader: We adore Thee, O Christ, and bless Thee.
All: Because by Thy holy cross Thou hast redeemed the world.

Jesus, you stand all alone before Pilate. Nobody speaks up for you. Nobody helps defend you. You devoted your entire life to helping others, listening to the smallest ones, caring for those who were ignored by others. They don't seem to remember that as they prepare to put you to death. As a child, sometimes I feel alone. Sometimes I feel that others don't stand up for me and defend me when I am afraid. Sometimes I don't feel like I am treated fairly, especially if I am scolded or corrected.

As an adult, sometimes I feel abandoned and afraid as well. Sometimes I too, feel like I am treated unfairly or blamed for things unfairly. I have a hard time when people criticize me at home or at work.

Help me be grateful for what you did for me. Help me to accept criticism and unfairness as you did, and not complain. Help me pray for those who have hurt me.

My Jesus, often have I signed the death warrant by my sins; save me by Thy death from that eternal death which I have so often deserved.

Our Father.... Hail Mary.... Glory Be to the Father....

Leader: Jesus Christ Crucified.

All: Have mercy on Us.

Leader: May the souls of the faithful departed, through the mercy of God, Rest in peace.

All: Amen.

2. *He is made to bear his cross*

Jesus, as you accepted your cross, you knew you would carry it to your death on Calvary. You knew it wouldn't be easy, but you accepted it and carried it just the same.

Leader: We adore you, O Christ, and we praise you.

All: Because by your holy cross You have redeemed the world.

Jesus, as you accepted your cross, you knew you would carry it to your death on Calvary. You knew it wouldn't be easy, but you accepted it and carried it just the same.

As a child, sometimes I don't like the problems that come my way. Sometimes I try to get others to take care of them or solve them for me. Sometimes I become upset and crabby when I'm asked to do even the smallest thing to help others. As an adult I sometimes feel like I'm not appreciated. Sometimes I feel as if I accept more responsibility that I need to. I can feel sorry for myself, even though the crosses others carry are much larger than my own. In my self-pity, I don't reach out to help.

My Jesus, Who by Thine own will didst take on Thee the most heavy cross I made for Thee by my sins, oh, make me feel their heavy weight, and weep for them ever while I live.

Our Father.... Hail Mary.... Glory Be to the Father....

Leader: Jesus Christ Crucified.

All: Have mercy on Us.

Leader: May the souls of the faithful departed, through the mercy of God, Rest in peace.

All: Amen.

3. *He falls the first time*

Jesus, the cross you have been carrying is very heavy. You are becoming weak and almost ready to faint, and you fall down. Nobody seems to want to help you. The soldiers are interested in getting home, so they yell at you and try to get you up and moving again.

Leader: We adore you, O Christ, and we praise you.

All: Because by your holy cross You have redeemed the world.

Jesus, the cross you have been carrying is very heavy. You are becoming weak and almost ready to faint, and you fall down. Nobody seems to want to help you. The soldiers are interested in getting home, so they yell at you and try to get you up and moving again.

As a child, sometimes I start to do something, but then get tired of it. I hurry to get finished and sometimes don't do my work well. Sometimes I don't pay attention to what I should be doing. When things get hard for me, sometimes I give up. As an adult, I sometimes put things off. I give up too easily, and sometimes don't do my work as well as I know I can.

My Jesus, the heavy burden of my sins is on Thee, and bears Thee down beneath the cross. I loathe them, I detest them; I call on Thee to pardon them; may Thy grace aid me never more to commit them.

Our Father.... Hail Mary.... Glory Be to the Father....

Leader: Jesus Christ Crucified.

All: Have mercy on Us.

Leader: May the souls of the faithful departed, through the mercy of God, Rest in peace.

All: Amen.

4. *He meets his mother*

Jesus, you feel so alone with all those people yelling and screaming at you. You don't like the words they are saying about you, and you look for a friendly face in the crowd. You see your mother. She can't make the hurting stop, but it helps to see that she is on your side, that she is suffering with you. She does understand and care.

Leader: We adore you, O Christ, and we praise you.

All: Because by your holy cross You have redeemed the world.

Jesus, you feel so alone with all those people yelling and screaming at you. You don't like the words they are saying about you, and you look for a friendly face in the crowd. You see your mother. She can't make the hurting stop, but it helps to see that she is on your side, that she is suffering with you. She does understand and care.

As a child, sometimes I feel like too many things are going on. Sometimes other kids pick on me and call me names. I need to look around me for a friendly face, and for the help I need. I need to share my troubles with those who truly care about me.

As an adult I sometimes feel overwhelmed by many things. Life is so competitive, and I worry so much about my future and those who have some control over it. I need to remember that being an adult does not mean having to solve every problem all by myself. I need to look around me for a friendly face, for the help I need.

Jesus most suffering, Mary Mother most sorrowful, if, by my sins, I caused you pain and anguish in the past, by God's assisting grace it shall be so no more; rather be you my love henceforth till death.

Our Father.... Hail Mary.... Glory be to the Father....

Leader: Jesus Christ Crucified.

All: Have mercy on Us.

Leader: May the souls of the faithful departed, through the mercy of God, Rest in peace.

All: Amen.

5. *Simon of Cyrene is made to bear the cross*

Jesus, the soldiers are becoming impatient. This is taking longer than they wanted it to. They are afraid you won't make it to the hill where you will be crucified. As you grow weaker, they grab a man out of the crowd and make him help carry your cross. He was just watching what was happening, but all of a sudden he is helping you carry your cross.

Leader: We adore you, O Christ, and we praise you.
All: Because by your holy cross You have redeemed the world.

Jesus, the soldiers are becoming impatient. This is taking longer than they wanted it to. They are afraid you won't make it to the hill where you will be crucified. As you grow weaker, they grab a man out of the crowd and make him help carry your cross. He was just watching what was happening, but all of a sudden he is helping you carry your cross.

As a child, sometimes I see people who need my help. Sometimes I pretend not to hear when my parents call me. I disappear when I know others could use my help.

As an adult, sometimes I try to do as little as I can and still get by. Others might need my help, but I ignore their needs. Even when I'm asked to help, I sometimes claim to be too busy.

My Jesus, blest, thrice blest was he who aided Thee to bear the cross. Blest too shall I be if I aid Thee to bear the cross, by patiently bowing my neck to the crosses Thou shalt send me during life. My Jesus, give me grace to do so.

Our Father.... Hail Mary.... Glory be to the Father....
Leader: Jesus Christ Crucified.
All: Have mercy on Us.
Leader: May the souls of the faithful departed, through the mercy of God, Rest in peace.
All: Amen.

6. Veronica wipes Jesus' face

Jesus, suddenly a woman comes out of the crowd. Her name is Veronica. You can see how she cares for you as she takes a cloth and begins to wipe the blood and sweat from your face. She can't do much, but she offers what little help she can.

Leader: We adore you, O Christ, and we praise you.
All: Because by your holy cross You have redeemed the world.

Jesus, suddenly a woman comes out of the crowd. Her name is Veronica. You can see how she cares for you as she takes a cloth and begins to wipe the blood and sweat from your face. She can't do much, but she offers what little help she can.

As a child, sometimes I know someone could use a little help and understanding. They may be picked on or teased by others, or just sad or lonely. Sometimes I feel bad that others don't step in to help, but I don't help either.

As an adult, I notice the needs around me. Sometimes my own family members crave my attention, and I don't even seem to notice. Sometimes a co-worker, friend, or family member could use help or understanding, but I don't reach out to help lest I be criticized, or that they demand more of me than I'd like to give.

My tender Jesus, Who didst deign to print Thy sacred face upon the cloth with which Veronica wiped the sweat from off Thy brow, print in my soul deep, I pray Thee, the lasting memory of Thy bitter pains.

Our Father.... Hail Mary.... Glory be to the Father....
Leader: Jesus Christ Crucified.
All: Have mercy on Us.
Leader: May the souls of the faithful departed, through the mercy of God, Rest in peace.
All: Amen.

7. *He falls the second time*

This is the second time you have fallen on the road. As the cross grows heavier and heavier it becomes more difficult to get up. But you continue to struggle and try until you're up and walking again. You don't give up.

Leader: We adore you, O Christ, and we praise you.
All: Because by your holy cross You have redeemed the world.

This is the second time you have fallen on the road. As the cross grows heavier and heavier it becomes more difficult to get up. But you continue to struggle and try until you're up and walking again. You don't give up.
As a child, sometimes things get me down. Others seem to find things easier to do or to learn. Each time I fail, I find it harder to keep trying.
As an adult, sometimes I think I should know more than I do. I become impatient with myself and find it hard to believe in myself when I fail. It is easy to despair over small things, and sometimes I do.
Help me when things seem difficult for me. Even when it's hard, help me get up and keep trying as you did. Help me do my best without comparing myself with others.
My Jesus, often have I sinned and often, by sin, beaten Thee to the ground beneath the cross. Help me to use the efficacious means of grace that I may never fall again.

Our Father.... Hail Mary.... Glory be to the Father....
Leader: Jesus Christ Crucified.
All: Have Mercy on Us.
Leader: May the souls of the faithful departed, through the mercy of God, Rest in peace.
All: Amen.

8. The women of Jerusalem weep over Jesus

Jesus, as you carry your cross you see a group of women along the road. As you pass by you see they are sad. You stop to spend a moment with them, to offer them some encouragement. Although you have been abandoned by your friends and are in pain, you stop and try to help them.

Leader: We adore you, O Christ, and we praise you.
All: Because by your holy cross You have redeemed the world.

Jesus, as you carry your cross you see a group of women along the road. As you pass by you see they are sad. You stop to spend a moment with them, to offer them some encouragement. Although you have been abandoned by your friends and are in pain, you stop and try to help them. As a child, sometimes I think a lot about myself. I think about what I want and would like people to spend their lives pleasing me.

As an adult, sometimes I act like a child. I become so absorbed in myself and what I'd like that I forget about the needs of others. I take them for granted, and often ignore their needs.

Help me think more about others. Help me remember that others have problems, too. Help me respond to them even when I'm busy or preoccupied with my own problems.

My Jesus, Who didst comfort the pious women of Jerusalem who wept to see Thee bruised and torn, comfort my soul with Thy tender pity, for in Thy pity lies my trust. May my heart ever answer Thine.

Our Father.... Hail Mary.... Glory be to the Father....
Leader: Jesus Christ Crucified.
All: Have Mercy on Us.
Leader: May the souls of the faithful departed, through the mercy of God, Rest in peace.
All: Amen.

9. *He falls the third time*

Jesus, your journey has been long. You fall again, beneath your cross. You know your journey is coming to an end. You struggle and struggle. You get up and keep going.

Leader: We adore you, O Christ, and we praise you.
All: Because by your holy cross You have redeemed the world.

Jesus, your journey has been long. You fall again, beneath your cross. You know your journey is coming to an end. You struggle and struggle. You get up and keep going.
As a child, sometimes I fail time and time again. I find it hard to get along with my sisters and brothers, sometimes I'm not honest, sometimes I'm lazy. I'm tempted to stop trying. It's just too hard sometimes.
As an adult, I often feel I should have conquered my weaknesses by now. I become discouraged when I'm confronted by the same problems over and over again. Sometimes I get weary. When I have health problems, I can become discouraged and depressed.
Help me think of the cross you carried. Help me continue to hope that I can make the changes in my life I need to. You didn't give up. I can have the strength to get up again as well.
My Jesus, by all the bitter woes Thou didst endure when for the third time the heavy cross bowed Thee to the earth, never, I beseech Thee, let me fall again into sin. Ah, my Jesus, rather let me die than ever offend Thee again.

Our Father.... Hail Mary.... Glory be to the Father....
Leader: Jesus Christ Crucified.
All: Have mercy on Us.
Leader: May the souls of the faithful departed, through the

mercy of God, Rest in Peace.
All: Amen.

10. *He is stripped of his garments*

The soldiers notice you have something of value. They remove your cloak and throw dice for it. Your wounds are torn open once again. Some of the people in the crowd make fun of you. They tease you and challenge you to perform a miracle for them to see. They're not aware that you'll perform the greatest miracle of all!

Leader: We adore you, O Christ, and we praise you.
All: Because by your holy cross You have redeemed the world.

The soldiers notice you have something of value. They remove your cloak and throw dice for it. Your wounds are torn open once again. Some of the people in the crowd make fun of you. They tease you and challenge you to perform a miracle for them to see. They're not aware that you'll perform the greatest miracle of all!
As a child, sometimes I'm tempted to repeat stories I know are unclean and disrespectful. I sometimes try to act grown up by using crude and bad words.
As an adult, sometimes I repeat stories that are disrespectful of others. I can entertain thoughts that are not clean. Sometimes I give the young people around me a bad example to follow.
Help me to keep myself pure and clean. Help me say things that build up the people around me. Help me overcome worldly desires that I may become more like Jesus. Help me set a good example for others to follow.
My Jesus, stripped of Thy garments and drenched with gall, strip me of love for things of earth, and make me loathe all

that savors of the world and sin.

Our Father.... Hail Mary.... Glory be to the Father....
Leader: Jesus Christ Crucified.
All: Have mercy on Us.
Leader: May the souls of the faithful departed, through the mercy of God, Rest in peace.
All: Amen.

11. *He is nailed to the cross*

You are stretched out on the cross you have carried so far. The soldiers take big nails and drive them into your hands and feet. You feel abandoned by the people you loved so much. People seem to have gone mad. You have done nothing but good, yet they drive nails through your hands and feet.

Leader: We adore you, O Christ, and we praise you.
All: Because by your holy cross You have redeemed the world.

You are stretched out on the cross you have carried so far. The soldiers take big nails and drive them into your hands and feet. You feel abandoned by the people you loved so much. People seem to have gone mad. You have done nothing but good, yet they drive nails through your hands and feet.

As a child, sometimes I hurt others. Sometimes I join with friends and decide not to like another. We gang up against another and cause them hurt and pain. Sometimes I say or do hurtful things to my brothers and sisters. I can wonder what they'd think about themselves if they believed everything I told them about themselves.

As and adult, sometimes I discriminate against others. Even without thinking, I judge others because of their color, intelligence, income level or name. I forget that I am to live as a brother or sister to all people. Sometimes I use harsh words when I speak to my children and family members. I can find it easy to look for something that isn't very important and make it very important.

Help me look again at the people around me. Help me see the hurt and pain I have caused in others. Be with me to help me make amends for the harm I have done.

My Jesus, by Thine agony when the cruel nails pierced Thy tender hands and feet and fixed them to the cross, make me crucify my flesh by Christian penance.

Our Father.... Hail Mary.... Glory be to the Father....

Leader: Jesus Christ Crucified.

All: Have mercy on Us.

Leader: May the souls of the faithful departed, through the mercy of God, Rest in peace.

All: Amen.

12. *He dies on the cross*

As Jesus hung on the cross, he forgave the soldiers who had crucified him, and prayed for his mother and friends. Jesus wanted all of us to be able to live forever with God, so he gave all he had for us.

Leader: We adore you, O Christ, and we praise you.

All: Because by your holy cross You have redeemed the world.

As Jesus hung on the cross, he forgave the soldiers who had crucified him, and prayed for his mother and friends. Jesus wanted all of us to be able to live forever with God, so he gave all he had for us.

Jesus, let me take a few moments now to consider your love for me. Help me thank you for your willingness to go to your death for me. Help me express my love for you!

My Jesus, three hours didst Thou hang in agony, and then die for me; let me die before I sin, and if I live, live for Thy love and faithful service.

Our Father.... Hail Mary.... Glory be to the Father....

Leader: Jesus Christ Crucified.

All: Have mercy on Us.

Leader: May the souls of the faithful departed, through the mercy of God, Rest in peace.

All: Amen.

13. *He is taken down from the cross*

Jesus, how brutally you were put to death. How gently your are taken from the cross. Your suffering and pain are ended, and you are put in the lap of your mother. The dirt and blood are wiped away. You are treated with love.

Leader: We adore you, O Christ, and we praise you.

All: Because by your holy cross You have redeemed the world.

Jesus, how brutally you were put to death. How gently your are taken from the cross. Your suffering and pain are ended, and you are put in the lap of your mother. The dirt and blood are wiped away. You are treated with love.

As a child, sometimes I treat others better when they're sad or in pain. When somebody dies, I become very gentle and kind. I notice the good and kind things people say about those who have died.

As an adult, I seem to be kinder when someone dies. If only I could learn to see the good things about them while they were alive. If only I would tell those around me how much I love them, while I still have the opportunity to do so.

Help me look for the good in those around me, especially

those I love the most. Help me live this day as if it were the last. Help me become a more gentle and loving person through my greater appreciation for those around me.

O Mary, Mother most sorrowful, the sword of grief pierced thy soul when thou didst see Jesus lying lifeless on thy bosom; obtain for me hatred of sin because sin slew thy Son and wounded thine own heart, and grace to live a Christian life and save my soul.

Our Father.... Hail Mary.... Glory be to the Father....

Leader: Jesus Christ Crucified.

All: Have mercy on Us.

Leader: May the souls of the faithful departed, through the mercy of God, Rest in peace.

All: Amen.

14. *He is placed in the sepulchre.*

Jesus, your body is prepared for burial. Joseph gave you his own tomb. He laid your body there and rolled a large stone in front of it, then went home. What a sad day it has been for so many people.

Leader: We adore you, O Christ, and we praise you.

All: Because by your holy cross You have redeemed the world.

Jesus, your body is prepared for burial. Joseph gave you his own tomb. He laid your body there and rolled a large stone in front of it, then went home. What a sad day it has been for so many people.

As a child, sometimes I try to keep everything for myself. I find it hard to share my things with my brothers or sisters and with my friends.

As an adult, I can be selfish too. I can accumulate things and keep them for myself. I try to make sure I have what I want before I share what I have with anybody else.

Help me think of Joseph of Arimathea, who risked his own life as he accepted Jesus' body for burial. Help me think of how Joseph loved Jesus so much that he gave him his own tomb.

My Jesus, beside Thy body in the tomb I, too, would lie dead; but if I live, let it be for Thee, so as one day to enjoy with Thee in heaven the fruits of Thy passion and Thy bitter death.

Our Father.... Hail Mary.... Glory be to the Father....

Leader: Jesus Christ Crucified.

All: have mercy on Us.

Leader: May the souls of the faithful departed, through the mercy of God, Rest in peace.

All: Amen.

Sacred Prayer to the Cross

The Cross is a great contradiction. A simple upright post with a transverse bar used crucifixion. It's a symbol of death, but so much more. Death and life, hate and love, violence and peace, accusation and forgiveness, sin and purity, brokenness and wholeness, all is lost yet everything is gained, destruction and restoration, defeat and victory. Once the cruelest form of execution, yet now it is a symbol of abundant life.

The Cross means many things to many people. Some have it displayed on their mantel, others wear it around their neck.

12

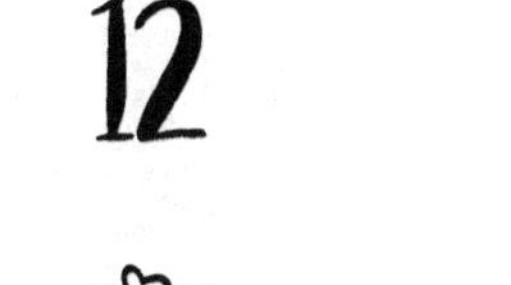

SACRED PRAYER

O! ADORABLE LORD AND SAVIOUR JESUS CHRIST DYING ON THE GALLOWS TRUE FOR OUR SINS. / O! HOLY CROSS OF JESUS SEE ME IN MY THOUGHTS / O! HOLY CROSS OF CHRIST WARD OFF FROM ME ALL WEAPONS OF DANGER. / O! HOLY CROSS OF CHRIST WARD OFF FROM ME ALL THINGS THAT ARE EVIL. / O! HOLY CROSS OF CHRIST PROTECT ME FROM MY ENEMIES. / O! HOLY CROSS / WARD OFF FROM ME ALL DANGEROUS DEATH / GIVE ME ALWAYS LIFE. / O! CRUCIFIED JESUS OF NAZARETH, I HAVE MERCY ON ME / NOW AND FOREVER / IN THE HONOUR OF OUR LORD JESUS CHRIST / AND IN THE HONOUR OF HIS SACRED PASSION / AND IN THE HONOUR OF HIS HOLY RESURRECTION / AND HIS GOD-LIKE ASCENSION / WHICH / HE LIKES TO BRING ME RIGHT INTO HEAVEN / TRUE AS JESUS CHRIST WAS BORN ON CHRISTMAS DAY / AND THE THREE WISE KINGS BROUGHT THEIR OFFERINGS ON THE 13TH DAY / TRUE AS JESUS CHRIST WAS CRUCIFIED ON MOUNT CALVARY ON GOOD FRIDAY / TRUE THAT NICODEMUS AND JOSEPH WHO TOOK OUR LORD DOWN FROM THE CROSS AND BURIED HIM. / AND TRUE AS HE ASCENDED INTO HEAVEN! SO THE HONOUR OF JESUS WILL KEEP ME FROM MY ENEMIES / VISIBLE / AND INVISIBLE NOW / AND FOREVER. / O! LORD JESUS CHRIST HAVE MERCY ON ME / MARY AND JOSEPH, PRAY FOR ME / O! LORD JESUS CHRIST, / THROUGH THY OWN SUFFERING FOR TRULY THY SOUL WAS PARTING OUT FROM THIS SINFUL WORLD. / GIVE GRACE THAT I MAY CARRY MY CROSS PATIENTLY / WITHOUT DREAD AND FEAR / WHEN I SUFFER / AND WITHOUT COMPLAINING / AND THAT THROUGH THY SUFFERINGS / I MAY ESCAPE ALL DANGERS NOW AND FOREVERMORE / AMEN. NOTE: THIS PRAYER WAS FOUND IN THE TOMB OF OUR LORD JESUS CHRIST IN THE YEAR 803 AND WAS SENT BY THE POPE TO EMPEROR CHARLES ON THE EVE OF HIS DEPARTURE TO BATTLE AND HE SENT IT TO ST. MICHAEL IN FRANCE WHOEVER READS OR WEARS THIS PRAYERS SHALL NEVER DIE A SUDDEN DEATH. BE BURNED, DROWNED NOR ANY POISON HAVE EFFECT ON HIM. HE WILL NEVER BE A PRISONER OF WAR; NOR BE VANQUISHED. WHEN A WOMAN LABOURS, LET HER WEAR IT ON HER RIGHT SIDE AND SHE WILL DELIVER SAFELY AND WHEN THE CHILD IS BORN, PIN THIS PRAYER ON HIS RIGHT SIDE HE SHALL NOT BE TROUBLED WITH ANY MISFORTUNE. AND BE SAFELY PRESERVED OF 82 ACCIDENTS. WHOEVER CARRIES THIS PRAYER WITH HIM, WILL NEVER HAVE ANY EPILEPTIC ATTACKS, AND IF YOU SEE ANY ONE IN FITS. PLACE THIS PRAYER ON ITS RIGHT SIDE, AND HE WILL BE CURED IMMEDIATELY AND THANK GOD. WHOEVER WRITES THIS PRAYER FOR HIMSELF OR FOR OTHERS WILL BE "BLESSED BY THE LORD." THEY WHO PRAY OR PLACE THIS PRAYER IN ANY HOUSE, WILL BE SAFELY GUARDED OF THUNDER AND LIGHTNING. BUT WHOEVER LAUGHS AT IT WILL SUFFER. BELIEVE THIS FOR CERTAIN. IT IS AS THE HOLY EVANGELIST HAD WRITTEN IT. WHOEVER PRAYS THIS PRAYER EVERYDAY FOR HIMSELF, SHALL HAVE THREE DAYS WARNING BEFORE HIS DEATH BY A HOLY SIGN.

The Divine Mercy Chaplet

The Chaplet of Mercy is recited using ordinary Rosary beads of five decades. The Chaplet is preceded by two opening prayers from the Diary of Saint Maria Faustina Kowalska and followed by a closing prayer.

13
The Chaplet

---

1. Make the Sign of the Cross

In the name of the Father, and of the Son, and of the Holy Spirit. Amen.

2. Optional Opening Prayers

St. Faustina's Prayer for Sinners

O Jesus, eternal Truth, our Life, I call upon You and I beg Your mercy for poor sinners. O sweetest Heart of my Lord, full of pity and unfathomable mercy, I plead with You for poor sinners. O Most Sacred Heart, Fount of Mercy from which gush forth rays of inconceivable graces upon the entire human race, I beg of You light for poor sinners. O Jesus, be mindful of Your own bitter Passion and do not permit the loss of souls redeemed at so dear a price of Your most precious Blood. O Jesus, when I consider the great price of Your Blood, I rejoice at its immensity, for one drop alone would have been enough for the salvation of all sinners. Although sin is an abyss of wickedness and ingratitude, the price paid for us can never be equalled. Therefore, let every soul trust in the Passion of the Lord, and place its hope in His mercy. God will not deny His mercy to anyone. Heaven and earth may change, but God's mercy will never be exhausted. Oh, what immense joy burns in my heart when I contemplate Your incomprehensible goodness, O Jesus! I desire to bring all sinners to Your feet that they may glorify Your mercy throughout endless ages.

You expired, Jesus, but the source of life gushed forth for souls, and the ocean of mercy opened up for the whole world. O Fount of Life, unfathomable Divine Mercy, envelop the whole world and empty Yourself out upon us.

(Repeat three times)
O Blood and Water, which gushed forth from the Heart of Jesus as a fount of mercy for us, I trust in You!

3. *Our Father*

Our Father, Who art in heaven, hallowed be Thy name; Thy kingdom come; Thy will be done on earth as it is in heaven. Give us this day our daily bread; and forgive us our trespasses as we forgive those who trespass against us; and lead us not into temptation, but deliver us from evil, Amen.

4. *Hail Mary*

Hail Mary, full of grace. The Lord is with thee. Blessed art thou amongst women, and blessed is the fruit of thy womb, Jesus. Holy Mary, Mother of God, pray for us sinners, now and at the hour of our death, Amen.

5. The Apostles' Creed

I believe in God, the Father almighty, Creator of heaven and earth, and in Jesus Christ, His only Son, our Lord, who was conceived by the Holy Spirit, born of the Virgin Mary, suffered under Pontius Pilate, was crucified, died and was buried; He descended into hell; on the third day He rose again from the dead; He ascended into heaven, and is seated at the right hand of God the Father almighty; from there He will come to judge the living and the dead. I believe in the Holy Spirit, the holy catholic Church, the communion of saints, the forgiveness of sins, the resurrection of the body, and life everlasting. Amen.

6. The Eternal Father

Eternal Father, I offer you the Body and Blood, Soul and Divinity of Your Dearly Beloved Son, Our Lord, Jesus Christ, in atonement for our sins and those of the whole world.

7. On the 10 Small Beads of Each Decade

For the sake of His sorrowful Passion, have mercy on us and on the whole world.

8. Repeat for the remaining decades

Saying the "Eternal Father" (6) on the "Our Father" bead and then 10 "For the sake of His sorrowful Passion" (7) on the following "Hail Mary" beads.

9. Conclude with Holy God (Repeat three times)

Holy God, Holy Mighty One, Holy Immortal One, have mercy on us and on the whole world.

10. Optional Closing Prayers

Eternal God, in whom mercy is endless and the treasury of compassion — inexhaustible, look kindly upon us and increase Your mercy in us, that in difficult moments we might not despair nor become despondent, but with great confidence submit ourselves to Your holy will, which is Love and Mercy itself.

O Greatly Merciful God, Infinite Goodness, today all mankind calls out from the abyss of its misery to Your mercy — to Your compassion, O God; and it is with its mighty voice of misery that it cries out. Gracious God, do not reject the prayer of this earth's exiles! O Lord, Goodness beyond our understanding, Who are acquainted with our misery through and through, and know that by our own power we cannot ascend to You, we implore You: anticipate us with Your grace and keep on increasing Your mercy in us, that we may faithfully do Your holy will all through our life and at death's hour. Let the omnipotence of Your mercy shield us from the darts of our salvation's enemies, that we may with confidence, as Your children, await Your [Son's] final coming — that day known to You alone. And we expect to obtain everything promised us by Jesus in spite of all our wretchedness. For Jesus is our Hope: through His merciful Heart, as through an open gate, we pass through to heaven.
Amen.

Catechism

A summary of the principles of Christian religion in the form of questions and answers, used for religious instruction.

14

1. The 10 Commandments

1. I am the Lord thy God! Thou shalt have no other Gods but me!
2. Thou shalt not take the Name of the Lord thy God in vain!
3. Thou shalt keep the Sabbath Day holy!
4. Thou shalt honor father and mother!
5. Thou shalt not kill!
6. Thou shalt not commit adultery!
7. Thou shalt not steal!
8. Thou shalt not bear false witness against thy neighbor!
9. Do not let thyself lust after thy neighbor's wife!
10. Thou shalt not covet thy neighbor's house, nor his farm, nor his cattle, nor anything that is his!

2. The Beatitudes

1. Blessed are the poor in spirit, for theirs is the kingdom of heaven.
2. Blessed are they who mourn, for they shall be comforted.
3. Blessed are the meek, for they shall inherit the earth.
4. Blessed are they who hunger and thirst for righteousness, for they shall be satisfied.

5. Blessed are the merciful, for they shall obtain mercy.
6. Blessed are the pure of heart, for they shall see God.
7. Blessed are the peacemakers, for they shall be called children of God.
8. Blessed are they who are persecuted for the sake of righteousness, for theirs is the kingdom of heaven.

3. The 2 Greatest Commandments

1. You shall love the Lord your God with all your heart, and with all your soul, and with all your mind.
2. You shall love your neighbor as yourself.

4. The 2 Principle mysteries of our Faith

1. Unity and Trinity of God
2. Incarnation, Passion, death, and Resurrection of our Lord

5. The 7 Sacraments

1. Baptism
2. Confirmation
3. Eucharist
4. Reconciliation
5. Anointing of the Sick
6. Matrimony
7. Holy Orders.

6. The 7 Gifts of the Holy Spirit

1. wisdom
2. understanding

3. counsel
4. fortitude
5. knowledge
6. piety
7. fear of the Lord.

7. The Charismatic Gifts of the Holy Spirit

1. the word of knowledge
2. increased faith
3. the gifts of healing
4. the gift of miracles
5. prophecy
6. the discernment of spirits
7. diverse kinds of tongues
8. interpretation of tongues.

8. The Fruits of the Holy Spirit

1. love
2. joy
3. peace
4. patience
5. kindness
6. generosity
7. faithfulness
8. gentleness
9. self-control

9. The 3 theological virtues

1. faith
2. hope

3. charity.

10. The 4 cardinal virtues

1. prudence
2. justice
3. fortitude
4. temperance.

11. The 7 Deadly Sins

1. pride
2. greed
3. lust
4. envy
5. gluttony
6. anger
7. sloth.

12. The 7 corporal works of Mercy

1. to feed the hungry
2. to give drink to the thirsty
3. to clothe the naked
4. to give shelter to travellers
5. to visit the sick
6. to visit the imprisoned
7. to bury the dead.

13. The 7 Spiritual works of Mercy

1. feeding the hungry
2. visiting the imprisoned

3. burying the dead
4. clothing the naked
5. caring for the sick
6. giving shelter to travelers
7. offering drink to the thirsty.

14. The Precepts of the Church

1. You shall attend Mass on Sundays and on holy days of obligation and rest from servile labor.
2. You shall confess your sins at least once a year.
3. You shall receive the sacrament of the Eucharist at least during the Easter season.
4. You shall observe the days of fasting and abstinence established by the Church.
5. You shall help to provide for the needs of the Church.

15. The 3 Essential Good Works

1. prayer
2. fasting
3. almsgiving

16. The 6 sins against the Holy Spirit

1. despair
2. presumption
3. impenitence
4. obstinacy
5. resisting divine truth
6. envy of another's spiritual welfare.

17. Conditions for Mortal Sin

1. grave matter
2. full knowledge
3. deliberate consent

18. 9 Ways we participate in other's sins

1. By Counsel
2. By Par-taking
3. By Consent
4. By Provocation
5. By Praise or Flattery
6. By Silence to Conceal the sin
7. By not Punish the Sinner
8. By Command or appeal/request
9. By Defence of the ill done

19. The 3 evangelical counsels

1. chastity
2. poverty
3. obedience.

20. The 3 Powers of the soul

1. the vegetative soul
2. the sentient soul
3. the rational soul

21. The 4 pillars of the church's authority

1. Creed
2. Prayer
3. Sacraments

4. Morality.

22. The 3 munera

1. Munus docendi (duty to teach, based on Christ's role as Prophet)
2. Munus sanctificandi (duty to sanctify, based on Chris's role as Priest)
3. Munus regendi (duty to shepherd, based on Christ's role as King)

23. The 3 parts of the church

1. Militant
2. Penitent
3. Triumphant.

24. The 4 marks of the church

1. one
2. holy
3. catholic
4. apostolic

25. The 9 choirs of Angels

1. Seraphim
2. Cherubim
3. Thrones
4. Dominations
5. Powers
6. Virtues
7. Principalities

8. Archangels
9. Angels

Biblical Facts

Bible, the sacred scriptures of Judaism and Christianity.

15

1. Every year, the Holy Bible sells over 100 million copies.
2. Non-profit organizations give out free Bibles all over the world.
3. The Bible has been translated to over 690 languages.
4. Hebrew is the original language of the Bible.
5. The average Bible has 1,200 pages.
6. The Holy Bible has 2 core verses. There are 39 books in the Old Testament and 27 books in the New Testament.
7. The Bible is grouped into five classifications. The Holy Bible is a collection of many type of books – historical books, books of poetry, prophetic books, epistles and the Gospels.
8. The Bible has 17 historical books
9. The Bible has 5 poetical books.
10. The Bible has 17 prophetic books.
11. The Bible has 4 Gospels.
12. The Bible has 21 Epistles.
13. There are 40 authors in the Bible.
14. The term "Bible" comes from the Greek word "Ta Biblia."
15. "Mahershalalhashbaz" is the longest word in the Bible.
16. It took over 1,000 years to complete the Old Testament.
17. The major religions follow the Old Testament.
18. Studies suggest that Islam originated from Ishmael.

19. There are only twelve prophets in the Bible.

20. The first Bibles did not have verses.

21. The Bible does not take account of the numbers of women and children.

22. Women spoke a total of 14,056 words in the Bible.

23. The smallest Bible is smaller than the tip of a pen.

24. The Bible has over 6,000 prophecies.

25. The world's most "stolen book" is the Bible.

26. 'Amen' is the Last word of the Bible.

27. In the Old Testament, the Bible has 39 books.

28. The New Testament has 27 books.

29. The Old Testament has the sacred scriptures of the Jewish faith.

30. The New Testament is the fulfillment of the prophecies of the Old Testament.

31. Written as early as 1200 BC, the Old Testament is the oldest book.

32. The apostles and missionaries wrote the New Testament in the first century AD.

33. Moses wrote the first five books of the Bible: Genesis, Exodus, Leviticus, Numbers, and Deuteronomy.

34. The Bible is over 3,000 years old.

35. In contrast to science, the Bible says that the earth is only 6,000 years old.

36. The Bible has more than 780,000 words.

37. The shortest verse in the Bible is John 11:35 – "Jesus wept."

38. Esther 8:9 is the longest verse in the Bible.

39. Psalm 119 is the longest chapter in the Bible.

40. There are 1,189 chapters in the Bible with 31,102 verses.

41. Methuselah is the oldest person in the Bible who died at the age of 969.

42. The Bible was written in three languages. Those languages are Hebrew, Aramaic, and Greek.

43. The longest book of the Bible is Psalms.

44. The shortest book of the Bible is 3 Joh

45. The Bible was written by more than 40 traditional authors

46. The Bible was written by people from diverse occupational backgrounds

47. The books of the Old Testament are arranged differently in Judaism

48. There are at least 185 songs in the Bible

49. Some of the "First" and "Second" books were divided after they were written

50. The authorship of Hebrews has remained anonymous for centuries

51. The word "Trinity" is never mentioned in the Bible

52. The Bible was written on three continents

53. There are 21 dreams recorded in the Bible

54. The book of James is the bossiest book of the Bible

55. The Bible is Over 1,000 Chapters Long. 1,189 chapters, with 929 in the Old Testament and 260 in the New Testament.

56. Jesus Is Never Described in Detail

57. The Geneva Bible Was the First to Be Printed on a Printing Press

58. The full Bible has been translated into 532 languages. It has been partially translated into 2,883 languages.

59. The longest chapter in the Bible is Psalm 119.

60. The shortest chapter in the Bible is Psalm 117, with just 2 verses

61. No original writings of the Bible exits.

62. No original writings of the Bible exits.

63. The word "Christ" is from the Greek khristos, meaning "the anointed," which is the noun of the verbal adjective khriein, meaning, "to rub anoint."

64. Nearly all of the villians in the Bible have red hair.
65. In the Old Testament, there are 23,145 verses. In the New Testament, there are 7, 957, for a total of 31,102 versus.
66. The toughest biblical heroine, it's got to be Judith.
67. The Bible's most married man was King Soloman.
68. The Bible indicates that the Earth is round in Isaiah 40:21-22.
69. The Book of Esther is the only book in the Bible that does not mention God's name.
70. The first gospel was written after almost 40 years of Jesus's death.